SEO

FUNDAMENTALS

AN INTRODUCTORY COURSE TO THE WORLD OF SEARCH ENGINE OPTIMIZATION

R.L. Adams

R.L. ADAMS

All Rights Reserved

FTC & Legal Notices

TABLE OF CONTENTS

SEO UNIVERSITY?

Whether you're new to the SEO industry, or have some knowledge under your belt, this series of courses has been designed to help guide you along your SEO educational career. Whether you've just launched a site, you're planning to launch one, you have an existing site that you need help ranking with, or you just want to understand how the convoluted field of SEO works, then the SEO University is for you. Beginning with the foundational understanding of SEO that you'll find in this particular course, *SEO Fundamentals,* you'll gain an understanding of the core concepts and principles that are involved with ranking with SEO today. You'll walk through not only the fundamentals of the SEO industry in this course, but also be introduced to what it takes to rank at the top of Google's search results.

With so much competition out on the Web, ranking at the top of Google's coveted searches is becoming increasingly difficult. If you've had any exposure to the field of SEO, then you know just how true this statement is. And, over the course of the past few years, we've seen Google institute some drastic changes to its algorithms. These changes have created catastrophic confusion amongst the SEO world since so much of what it takes to rank today is different than it was just a few short years ago. So, in order to manage the tangled Web that Google has woven, it's important to have an understanding of the fundamentals for ranking, and just what it's going to take to propel your Website to the top of Google's search results. That's what this particular course is designed to give you.

Once you have a solid grasp of the fundamentals involved with the SEO industry, you can then progress to understanding and implementing some of the advanced strategies and tactics being used by top online marketers to rank their sites today. However, so much goes into ranking at the top of Google's search results. So much in fact, that oftentimes those same top online marketers won't reveal to you just how much time and effort it takes to rank a particular site at the top of Google's search results. Furthermore, since Google wants to show its users the best listings at the top, and since there are only 10 listings on that first page, competition is fierce no matter what anyone tells you. Most keywords have millions of people competing for them so the stakes are high. To the victor go the spoils, and there are no better spoils than virtually limitless free organic search traffic from Google.

That's why SEO education is paramount.

Without educating yourself on just how to rank today, you'll miss the opportunity for driving all of that free organic search traffic your way. And, without free organic search traffic, you'll be left scrambling to find other paid ways to drive traffic to your site. And, it's clear that most of us don't have limitless marketing budgets, so we must put in the time and effort associated with SEO. But, before we can begin marketing like a seasoned SEO professional, we all have to start somewhere, and that somewhere is by first understanding the fundamentals that are involved in the field of SEO. And, that's precisely what this particular course is designed to help you do. Once you've developed that foundational understanding, you can move on to the subsequent courses in the SEO University.

So, What Exactly is the SEO University?

So, what exactly is the SEO University, and why should you care? Well, one of the most frustrating parts about launching any business, whether online or offline, lies in its marketing. Having the wherewithal and understanding to take a business from concept to fruition is one thing. But, actually getting people to know about that business and become paying customers or clients is an entirely different thing. And, to add insult to injury, marketing online is incredibly difficult when you don't have the proper understanding of just how the search engines work. Traditional marketing is one thing, and online marketing is an entirely different one. That's why SEO education is so important. Without the proper understanding, you could be left spinning your wheels, wondering why you're not making any progress.

From on-site optimization, to off-site optimization, to social media marketing, unique content creation, and everything in between, marketing on the Web is layered with challenges. From the terminology, to the steps required, and the generation of traffic, leads, and sales, the SEO University will show you just what it takes to take any business into the mainstream. No matter if you're a complete beginner, or you have an understanding of SEO, you'll learn the concept and principles it takes to market on the Web today. The SEO University goes beyond just the SEO fundamentals, which you'll learn in this particular course, and stems into actual strategies that you can implement today to give your business the kick-start it needs. Whether you're selling goods, services, or information, the knowledge contained in these courses will be vital to your success.

Once you've created a solid foundation by understanding the fundamentals of SEO, the other courses will assist you in really propelling your SEO career to the next level. For the time being, this course will help to lay the groundwork for what will surely be an exciting career in the SEO field. Once you've come to grasp all the important elements involved with SEO, you'll understand just how to implement some of the advanced strategies that will help you climb your way up the SEO ladder on Google's search results. The better you understand and grasp these concepts now, the easier it will be for you to propel your SEO career forward with the advanced strategies. Take the time to really understand just what's involved with the fundamentals before moving forward. If you're unclear of something, go back and read it again until you're confident and fully grasp it.

INTRODUCTION

What was once an SEO industry that was thriving at the behest of professional search engine spammers, has been flipped upside down, shaken, turned around, and left asunder. A virtual atomic bomb leveled the entire playing field, spreading its digital ashes in the vast arrays of cyberspace, to only be collected and pieced back together by the purveyors of the Web. So, what happened and why does this sound dramatic? Well, the SEO industry has seen an incredible amount of change, primarily due to one reason: relevancy. Google's desire for relevancy has been the major driving force behind all of the change – change that's benefited both sides of the coin.

On the one end, you've had the search engines that have been vying to provide better and far more accurate search results to its end users. The end users of Google are its customers, or the searchers for the matter. Whenever you go onto the Web, whether from a desktop, a laptop, a tablet, or a mobile device, and you conduct a search,

Google's mission is to provide you with the most relevant search results at the top of the list. It wants to ensure that you find what you're looking for, quickly and painlessly. The top ten listings on page one are designed with that particular mission in mind. Google wants the most relevant results at the top, and the least relevant results at the bottom. And, the bottom can stretch on and on for countless pages. The goal of course here is to be number one.

So, change has certainly benefited the end users. The changes that have been instituted by Google have been plentiful, but they've all had the end desire of increasing relevancy. Google wants the most relevant search results first, that's apparent. However, the other side of the coin has also seen some drastic changes that have benefited the Websites that are competing for rank. That's because, years back, search engine marketers were instituting something called Black-Hat SEO techniques in order to push certain listings up to the top of Google's search results. These listings may not have been the most relevant search results for specific keyword searches, but they were virtually forced to the top of Google's searches with the help of some now-illicit techniques.

Black-Hat SEO caused the industry to be flipped on its head. It angered Google because it was resulting in the loss of relevancy. When the top search results are manipulated so drastically, Google can no longer fulfill its mission of providing the most relevant search results, first. Because of these Black-Hat SEO techniques, Google made some changes. This is where the virtual atomic bomb comes into play. Those changes to its algorithm literally leveled the playing field. The algorithm changes have been plentiful, but they've all had the singular goal that's part of Google's overall mission, and that is to increase relevancy. And, now that Google's search algorithms have been readjusted, the listings that actually are the most relevant appear at the top of its search results.

Sound confusing?

Well, it is to a certain extent. However, you need not worry. We'll be covering all of these details and more in the coming sections of this course. This will provide you with an inherent understanding of not only how the search engine industry works, but how best to leverage certain best-practices to move your site up Google's search engine listings without getting penalized. There's so much to cover, so it's important that we get started. You can use the SEO University by reading through it from front to back, or jumping forward to the courses or sections that may best benefit you today.

1
GETTING STARTED WITH SEO

Before embarking on your SEO career, you have to understand the fundamentals first. These fundamentals will include industry-wide nomenclature, historical information about the SEO field, and basic principles involved with ranking today. If you already have a solid understanding of the fundamentals involved in SEO, then you should still briefly skim through the information. However, if you don't have a solid grasp on the fundamentals, it's important to study the information in this chapter with diligence. The fundamentals will be necessary in the wider understanding of advanced strategies and tactics that will be necessary to help you rank higher, consistently in the long term.

So, what are the fundamentals to SEO? Well, SEO is based on trust today – Google's trust that is. If Google can trust your site and your content, you'll be more likely to rank than if it doesn't do so. But building Google's trust is difficult. It involves complying with certain guidelines across multiple spectrums as it affects any Webpage. These three spectrums of trust have evolved over time with Google's algorithm. And, based on the changes it has made in ranking today, those three spectrums of trust have become much harder to artificially manipulate. Those three spectrums of trust are as follows:

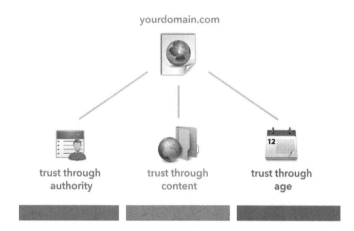

1. <u>Trust through Authority</u> – Authority relates to just how important Google sees a specific Webpage. If, for example, other Websites that Google already trusts have links to the Webpage, then it's trust in authority rank increases. The more Websites that link to the Webpage that Google already trusts, the higher the trust in authority becomes.

2. Trust through Content – On the Web, Google sees content as king. And, its recent algorithm adjustments have focused heavily on the quality of content, amongst other things. In order to create trust through content, you must be able to deliver unique, high-quality content on the Webpage that's well researched. Well-researched articles that answer specific questions have particular prominence here.

3. Trust through Age – This relates to the age of the domain name, but not when it was first registered. Trust in age relies on when Google first indexed a particular domain. This has an enormous impact on just how quickly new domain names can rank. New domain names will have difficulty ranking for even low-competition keywords because of an inability to satisfy the trust through age component.

Now, building trust across these three spectrums involves a lot of heavy lifting, so to speak. It also involves a careful balance between promoting, but not over promoting. If Google sees you trying to over-promote a Webpage, especially one that is relatively new and lacks authority, it will actually decrease the ranking of that listing. Yes, I know that it's a tough pill to swallow. But, these changes are a direct result of the problems that Google experienced in the past. When spammers took over most of Google's search results, it had to fight back in some way. In response, Google came up with a more intuitive way to determine search rankings. The result was a slew of algorithm changes dubbed names like Google Panda, Google Penguin, and more recently, Google

Hummingbird.

As Google fought back against all the spam and low-quality content sites on the Web, it instituted this multi-spectrum approach to ranking Webpages. Furthermore, it's now very difficult to bend the rules whatsoever, since Google tracks everything. It indexes a slew of data that includes very detailed information about any Webpage. From when it was first indexed, to the number of outbound links, the number of inbound links and the IP diversification of those links, the quality of content, information about the domain the Webpage is on, and so on. The new algorithm adjustments make it very difficult to cheat your way up to the top of Google's search results. So, you have to do the work. After you understand the fundamentals, we'll go into more detail about the specifics of ranking a piece of content while strictly adhering to the three factors of trust.

And, as you'll come to find, ranking a Webpage for a keyword search is going to take your ability to successfully weave together a multi-faceted approach based on the three factors of trust. You're going to have to be able to build trust by wearing many different hats. While it will be a difficult climb to the top of any of Google's search engine results pages, or SERPs, the rewards will be plentiful. When you can rank on the first page of results for any SERP, the amount of traffic that you can potentially generate is limitless. Furthermore, once you've built trust along the three spectrums of trust for your site, by constantly adding more unique and well-researched content to your site, you'll be able to increase that trust even more. But we have to start somewhere.

So, before we delve too deep into specific discussions about SEO tactics, it's important to first understand the evolution of how these present spectrums of trust came about. In essence, Google's goal has always been to provide its users with the best and most relevant answers to their search queries. As the Web grew and expanded over the years, things got a little bit out of hand when rogue search engine marketers, or SEMs, set out to create poorly-written content, amongst other things, that was intended to spam Google's search engine to help increase ranks of certain sites. Google eventually caught on, and began instituting updates to its algorithm. Each algorithm update Google has instituted, from the Panda, to the Penguin, to the Exact Match Domain (EMD) update, and now to the Hummingbird, has had the ultimate aim of providing increasingly relevant search results.

So, in order to win the game of search on Google today, and appear within the first page of its SERPs, you must have a Webpage that successfully addresses all three spectrums of trust. Of course, you must have high-quality content that is unique and provides value. But the other two factors of trust must be present as well. However, when the content is unique, people will inherently share that content, helping you to create trust through authority. Think about it for a moment. Let's say you find an amazing blog post somewhere on the Web, then share it on Facebook. That share, then gets re-shares many times over, likes, tweets, and then begins to make its rounds on the Web. What do you think will happen to that piece of content? It will begin to rank high, that's what.

As long as the other factors of trust are addressed, a piece of content that is unique and provides value, which is actively shared around the Web, is going to increase in rank. Not only will the Webpage increase in rank, but also as a result, so will the domain name in question. As long as the domain name has some trust in age (we'll get to what exactly this means), then the content will begin topping Google's SERPs for its intended keyword search. Yes, so much more goes on between the sheets. So many different factors come into play when sculpting that content. But the quality of the content is so critical; it's foundational. So, it's important to always create high-quality content when fashioning anything on the Web. Too many SEMs focus on releasing low-quality content, and it stings when it comes time to rank. Don't fall into this trap.

GOOGLE'S ALGORITHM UPDATES: AN OVERVIEW

One of the important fundamentals of the SEO trade is gaining an inherent understanding to Google's algorithm updates that have leveled the playing field. By understanding these changes, you can better understand the mindset of the Google search engine. And, when you have an understanding of the mindset of the Google search engine, you can more accurately tailor your content to fall inline with just what Google wants. Possessing this knowledge is paramount for anyone looking to truly understand SEO since it presents the current environment through perspective lens of evolutionary progress in search.

Now, you might also be asking yourself, "Why only the focus on Google?" Why don't we focus on other search engines? Well, as we've seen over the past two decades, search engines have come and gone. But, Google's search has arrived and it's here to stay. Through its far reach on the Web, Google is playing a larger role every single day in our lives. Through the launch of free services such as Gmail, Google Plus, and Google Maps, it has entrenched itself in the lives of billions of people around the world. And, according to a July 2013 comScore Study, Google's share of search is now at 67%, with Microsoft's Bing, Yahoo, Ask Network, and AOL, trailing far behind with 17.9%, 11.3%, 2.7%, and 1.2% respectively.

With such an enormous lead on its rivals, it's no wonder why Google is the be-all and end-all when it comes to online search. And, it's by far one of the most forward-thinking search engines on the Web today, working diligently to provide higher relevancy search results every single day. Due to its obsession over enhancing its user-experience and its accuracy in relevant organic search results, so many people around the world trust only Google for their searches across multiple platforms. So, in order to understand just how relevant Google wants its search results to be, we have to look at the evolution of its algorithm. Of course, any algorithm is going to change over time, as it's in the nature of progress and innovation to make things better. But Google's changes have gone far and beyond a natural evolutionary progression. They've been drastic.

So, what's changed exactly?

Well, in the beginning, when Google first opened its virtual doors in 1996, its goal was to provide a better and more organic search for the Web. It wanted to catalog and index everything according to something that they coined PageRank, which is still in use today. In essence, PageRank is the importance attributed to a page based on Google's algorithm. Today, that algorithm is far different than it was back when they first started cranking the preverbal wheel.

Still, nonetheless, PageRank is the definition of how important a page is in the eyes of Google. It can range from as low as zero, to as high as ten. Websites like Google, Facebook, and YouTube take those top coveted rankings. And, any new site that is yet to be indexed, or is newly indexed, would take rankings such as zero or one.

We'll talk more about PageRank in the coming sections. However, for now, let's look at the different algorithms that have had some formidable effects on Google's search results.

1. <u>Google Panda</u> – The Google Panda was first introduced in February of 2011. This was a turning point for Google and a time when it began aggressively battling the massive amounts of spammers that were aiming to manipulate its search results. The focus of the Google Panda was on the user-browsing experience, and according to Google itself, it affected 12% of search results. But, the effects of Google Panda were widespread, and severely crippled the rankings of sites with thin content, content farms, sites that had high ad-to-content ratios, and other issues relating to the quality of the user-browsing experience.

2. <u>Google Penguin</u> – The Google Penguin was first rolled out in April of 2012, in response to Web-spam tactics that are now categorized as Black-Hat SEO techniques. This included, but wasn't limited to, things like keyword stuffing in meta tags, content cloaking, sneaky redirects, and other over-optimization techniques that were being implemented SEMs.

3. Exact Match Domains – Also known as EMDs, this algorithm update was rolled out in September of 2012 in an effort to tackle low-quality domain names that exactly match the keyword search, from appearing at the top of search results. This affected over 10% of EMDs, and were mainly focused on those that provided little to no value and unique content.

4. Google Hummingbird – This algorithm update was launched in August of 2013 and related to semantic searches and the Knowledge Graph. Google's aim with this algorithm update was to help better answer questions posed in searches by its end-users. It wants to provide higher-quality results and quicker answers for users searching for specific questions.

You might be asking yourself, "Why should I care about these algorithm updates? The past is the past, right?" Well, you have to care about these algorithm updates, because they've had a severe impact on search. And, what's more important, is just what these algorithm updates mean. No doubt, Google will certainly be releasing more updates in the future. In fact, it will continue to refine and tweak its algorithm. But it has always had one singular mission in mind: relevancy. When you realize the importance of this word, you'll be on your way to ranking higher over the long term. And, to be seen as more relevant, you have to ensure that anything you do on the

Web is natural, organic, and of the highest quality possible.

So, when you write a blog article, it has to be high quality. When you create authority links, they have to be high-quality links. When you do anything on the Web that relates to the optimization of your Webpage, it has to be high quality, always. When you don't adhere to this fundamental law of SEO, then your search rankings are surely going to suffer. If you do adhere to it, you can be sure that you'll be able to skyrocket any Webpage to the top of Google's SERPs over time. Just keep in mind that it's not going to happen overnight. Like anything else that's worthwhile in life, SEO takes a good amount of concerted effort applied consistently over time. Meaning, Google wants to see high-quality links being created to your content, not all at once, but naturally and over time. Since it tracks the number of links to your content and the days on which they were created, anything unnatural looking is going to get you penalized.

Over-optimization is another thing to be very careful of when working on SEO. If the algorithm updates can tell you anything beyond the fact that Google's mission is increased relevancy, it's that by trying to over-do relevancy, it's going to hurt you. This was one of the main objectives of the Google Penguin update, and its intended purpose was to penalize the over-optimizers of the Web. Now, even if you're new to SEO and you wouldn't dream of attempting to over-optimize a Webpage, you may end up doing it inadvertently. So, you have to be careful and pay extra attention to over-optimization while endeavoring in anything SEO related. In essence, you have to be able to walk that fine line between too much optimization and too little optimization. That fine line is Google's current tolerance level for both new and existing Websites.

2

THE GOOGLE MINDSET

What should be clear now is that SEO is built on a foundation of trust. The recent algorithm changes that Google implemented were meant to both enhance and preserve that trust. That's because Google was losing the relevancy battle on the Web. As professional SEMs continued to bend the rules, most of the top search results weren't necessarily the most relevant ones. However, today things are far different. The organic search results provided by Google have become even more accurate with each passing algorithm update. And, of course, that's Google's main goal: relevancy. So, if you want to adhere to Google's new rules, you must appear relevant. And, to appear relevant, Google must trust you.

So, trust is a core fundamental to SEO, and is needed as the foundation to any good optimization campaign; that much is clear. But, we all know that trust isn't built so easily. It takes a significant amount of backbreaking work to win Google's trust. Today, the search giant won't blindly trust sites as it once did; its trust must be earned. And, when most newcomers to the SEO world try to optimize a site, they usually concede in silent resignation. They tend to accept the fact that they will never be able to rank their sites high enough simply because they don't understand all the components involved with SEO. So, yes, SEO can be incredibly difficult to implement without the proper foundational understanding of what it takes to rank today.

So, how does this trust really work? Although I provided a brief overview of the different components of trust, let's take a look at just what it takes to earn Google's trust across the three spectrums. To recap on those spectrums, today, you'll need to earn Google's trust in age, content, and authority. But how is that done? How do you go about ensuring that you're trusted by Google and appear relevant in its eyes? Well, the road to earning Google's trust isn't an easy one; it's long and arduous. You'll have to ensure that certain criteria are first met so that you don't end up in Google's Sandbox, a place where Websites go that are new or misbehaving.

What's the Google Sandbox?

One of the fundamental aspects to be aware of when conducting SEO is Google's Sandbox. So, what is the Google Sandbox exactly? Also known as the Google Penalty, Sandboxing, or the Sandbox Effect, the Google Sandbox is a place where Websites go that don't have, or merely lose, Google's trust. And, although the existence of the Google Sandbox has never been publicly acknowledged or confirmed by Google, it's a real effect born due to Google's new rules. And, although some reports claim that this Google Penalty has existed as far back as 2004, it's only been until recently when its effects have been exaggerated. With the introduction of the recent algorithm adjustments, this Sandbox Effect has been something that SEMs must pay careful attention to.

So, what happens exactly when you're ensnarled in the Google Sandbox, and how do you go about avoiding becoming its next victim? Well, now that Google's SERPs are built more on trust ever than before, this Sandbox Effect is something that can significantly damage the rankings of a site if that trust is abused or is nonexistent in the first place. What does this mean? Well, there are several scenarios that we can liken the Google Sandbox to, which will help to better describe just how it works and how to avoid it. And, now that have a better idea of the three different spectrums of trust, you'll understand just how Google will use those spectrums of trust to decide which sites get penalized and which ones do not.

Scenario #1 – Brand New Domain Name

One of the most common scenarios that exist today, are SEMs who are attempting to rank Websites with brand-new domain names. Since trust through age is a vital component in rank today, new domain names will not receive the same level of trust that they once did with Google. In the past – before 2011 – it was relatively easy to register a new domain name, and quickly move it up the ranks of Google's SERPs. Professional SEMs would do this by instituting Black-Hat SEO techniques that would quickly propel the sites up the organic search listings. This was to the detriment of the other domains that were vying to compete, but using ethical techniques to rank through content and authority. They would build unique content and farm quality links across the Web, but would be outranked by sites that weren't necessarily playing by the rules, or bending them to say the least.

This was around the time that Google began making some major overhauls to its algorithms with the introduction of things like the Google Panda, then the Penguin. So, what the Panda and the Penguin achieved over time was the filtering of SEO practices. For example, certain links wouldn't be weighted as heavily as they normally would be, unique content wouldn't be ranked as high as it normally would be, and so on. This filtering effect affected new and existing sites immensely. However, when there was a new domain name, Google's new rules taught it to not trust that domain name, especially when it didn't have a lot of authority. This doesn't necessarily mean that new domain names can't rank high on Google's SERPs, but they won't rank *as high* if they don't collect some authority.

So, what does it mean to collect authority? Well, let's say for example there's a new domain name that's been in existence for less than a year. If that domain name has little authority, it will be incredibly difficult to have it rank high up on Google's SERPs. But, by building authority through the creation of high-quality links that link back to the domain name across the Web, it will rank higher, faster. Furthermore, if there are very prominent links that come back to that site, from other very trusted sites on the Web, then it will occur much faster. For example, if a prominent online media site or blog does an article about a site on a new domain name, it will propel it up the SERPs much faster. Sites like TechCrunch.com, Mashable.com, HuffingtonPost.com, or the NewYorkTimes.com, that link back to a new domain name, will add huge amounts of authority, or validity, in the eyes of Google.

However, usually, the case is that new domain names don't have a lot of authority. There aren't many trusted Websites linking back to that domain, generally. When this happens, Google refuses to trust that domain, placing it in its Sandbox. So, how long does this go on for? Well, there are no specific instructions on the Web that will provide you with the answer to this question. However, so many guestimates exist. Now, when we talk about the age of a domain name, this doesn't necessarily mean the date when it was first registered. No, this refers to the date that Google first found and indexed that domain name. That's why having a brand new domain name, never before registered and indexed by Google, can be so detrimental to the potential for ranking. It's far better to have a domain name that was once owned by someone else and indexed by Google in the past.

So, in the scenario of a new domain name, it's going to be difficult to rank. If you're stuck with a brand new domain name, your work is going to be considerably more arduous than if you were to have something called an aged domain name. What's an aged domain name? Well, we'll get into that later on along with the tactics that can be used to purchase and quickly rank one on Google to move up the SERPs far quicker than you would be able to with a non-aged domain name that's new. This is an important factor in rank and Sandboxing. By having an aged domain name, Google will be less likely to filter the effect of all your SEO work. That's why brand new domain names can be one of the most frustrating scenarios for SEMs and Website owners who try tirelessly to build authority and unique content, but can't seem to rank anywhere on Google's SERPs.

Scenario #2 – Penalized Domain Name

Another way to get your Website Sandboxed is by over-optimizing your domain name. Another of the direct cause-and-effect relationships that has arisen from the algorithm updates has been the indirect relationship between high rankings and over-optimization. The more you try to over-optimize a domain name, the less likely it's going to rank high for any given SERP. For this reason, it's important to be sensitive to over-optimization. And, while you can't specifically quantify what precisely over-optimization is going to mean to Google, you can come to some educated guestimates about it. What's important to keep in mind is that, if it doesn't seem organic and natural, Google is going to find out. However, there's also the flipside of that coin as well, because you'll want to achieve link diversity by having many very IP-diverse links out on the Internet.

However, for now, it's important to understand that you can quickly end up in Google's Sandbox is by over-optimizing your domain. Too much of one method is going to get you red-flagged. So, if you attempt to generate thousands of links or hundreds of links all from the same source each day, Google is going to know that something's just not right. And, if those links all contain the same keyword, then you're sure to get your site penalized. So, you have to ensure that you have a well-diverse campaign of high-quality profile links along with lower-quality links as well. And, the keywords contained in those links have to be diverse. Furthermore, if the content that the link stems from is high-quality content and unique, then it's even better. I know that this sounds like a lot to absorb in such a short period, but the more you understand these fundamentals, the easier your work is going to be later down the road.

But, over-optimizing isn't just something that's achieved with link bombardment. By creating hundreds or even thousands of links in such a short period, isn't the only thing that will get you penalized by Google. If the content that you create isn't unique, and for example is copied from other sources, this is also another sure way to get yourself into Google's Sandbox. Now, this doesn't mean that you can't quote from sources. I'm talking about the copying of entire articles verbatim from other Websites out on the Web. This would be betraying trust through content as opposed to betraying trust through authority. If you'll think about the three spectrums of trust, it's very easy to lose Google's trust by enacting these types of more illicit SEO activities. So, it's important to tread with caution here. Be very careful to not have your domain penalized by over-optimizing through link building or through content copying.

Once your domain name has been penalized and it enters into Google's Sandbox, it's very difficult to recover. You have to really work harder to gain or regain Google's trust, so it's best to try not to overdo it when working in SEO. This is probably one of the biggest mistakes made by newcomers to the field. Everyone wants to do everything that they can to ensure that they move their site up the rankings quickly, but they don't all necessarily understand the pitfalls associated with trying to force your way up. So, it's important to be aware of these pitfalls before setting out to engage in this type of work. Everyone gets extremely excited when they come upon a technique that they think might propel them up the rankings. But, it's important to understand that overdoing SEO can get you severely penalized. So, you must always keep the terms "natural and organic" in your mind, no matter what you do related to SEO.

Scenario #3 – Exact-Match Domain Names

I briefly discussed one of Google's recent algorithm updates entitled exact-match domains, or EMDs – another scenario that can find a domain's way into poor graces with Google. In the past, SEMs would register EMDs in an effort to quickly rank at the top of organic search results. For example, if you would take a search term such as "Best Acne Treatment Medicine," the EMD would be equivalent to BestAcneTreatmentMedicine.com. However, you can't merely go about purchasing EMDs in order to rank high for a given keyword search. If you try to do so, and the quality of the EMD is low, then you can expect to end up in the Google Sandbox. However, if the quality of the content and authority is high, the EMD should function as intended.

Many people still tout the EMD approach to quickly skyrocketing up Google's search results, but it doesn't always work that way. Today, there are so many Internet Marketers on the Web touting the secrets to making money online with Google, claiming to know just how to manipulate the system. But, their systems usually don't work out for people precisely the way in which they describe. That's because all three components of trust must exist for Google, and it's very hard to force Google's trust. It must happen over time, and be gradually built up. Google wants to see people putting in the effort and time, naturally creating high-quality content that other people link to. So, if you do decide to take the EMD approach, you have to go about conducting your SEO efforts just like you would any other domain name. But, with the EMD, you'll find quicker advances up Google's SERPs as long as you play by the rules and you don't try to do too much too fast.

However, all that being said, EMDs are an excellent way to approach creating niche Websites to sell products or services from. As long as the domain name exactly matches the keyword search, and the quality of the content and the authority is high, you'll fair better with an EMD than you will with a non-EMD for that particular keyword search. And, if the EMD is very high quality, it will generally rank for terms similar to its domain name. For example, if you were to build up a high-quality EMD for the keyword "iPhone 7 Rumors," then you might just be able to rank for the search term "iPhone Rumors" depending on how much authority and content you were to build up. Additionally, if the domain name is aged, then you'll do much better in the long term with many related searches that closely match that EMD. However, you must do things as naturally and organically as possible. There are ways you can slightly bend the rules here and there, but doing too much too fast will get you into hot water with the search giant.

3

BLACK, WHITE, AND GRAY

An important distinction to understand in the world of SEO is the difference between Black-Hat SEO, White-Hat SEO, and Gray-Hat SEO. The latter term, Gray-Hat SEO, is a term that I'm using here that will distinguish the mesh between both the Black-Hat SEO and White-Hat SEO camps. These would involve techniques that might slightly bend the rules a bit, but if conducted properly, won't find your domain name ending up in the Google Sandbox. So, what's the real difference namely between Black-Hat SEO and White-Hat SEO? And, why is this an important distinction to make?

The difference between Black-Hat SEO and White-Hat SEO is enormous. Specifically, in your quest to achieve SEO Mastery, it's important that you do your best to adhere to a White-Hat SEO set of guidelines. Now, later on, when you're a bit more comfortable with SEO and achieve a deeper understanding, you can delve into a Gray-Hat SEO practice, which combines some of the benefits of Black-Hat SEO in a White-Hat SEO organic fashion. Sound confusing? Well, don't worry; it will make much more sense here shortly. For now, it's important to understand that the White-Hat SEO practices are those that are acceptable use practices by Google in the field of SEO, and Black-Hat SEO practices are not.

So, what actually differentiates the worlds of SEO these days?

Well, whether we talk about Black-Hat, White-Hat, or Gray-Hat SEO, we're really talking about considerably different techniques. However, there is a foundational understanding of what must exist no matter what techniques you're going to employ. That foundation is quality content. When the underlying content is of high quality, a strong basis exists for moving that content up Google's SERPs. Gone are the days of being able to farm content, spin content, and create generally low-quality content specifically intended to gain rank. Today, Google wants very high-quality content in its attempts to increase the overall quality of the Web.

Look, whenever we search for content out there, we want to be able to find the most relevant content first. But what does that really mean? What does it mean to find relevant content that answers the questions that we're seeking to find the answers for? This is something important that you'll need to ask yourself. If you're producing content solely for the purposes of ranking high, then you won't see yourself succeeding if you don't work to create content that provides value. When you add value Google takes notice. And, adding value should be at the foundation of everything that you do. It shouldn't just be about the all-mighty dollar. Rather, the dollar, or profit if you may, should be secondary to the desire to create value. And, that value can come in many different forms, but the best kind of value you can provide to the web is well-researched and well-written content that fills a specific need.

The Game of Semantics

An important fundamental understanding that you must come to is the fact that Google is now moving away from full keyword-driven search and more towards semantic searches. What does this mean? Well, first off, semantics is the science of how words within phrases relate to one another. For example, if you were to ask certain questions about conversions between units such as kilograms and pounds, you'll notice that Google will now provide you with the answer above the search results. Google's purpose is to answer your question as quickly and as efficiently as possible. And, if it can understand just what you're asking it, it wants to be able to provide that answer at the very top of its search results.

This continues with Google's ultimate goal to provide the most relevant search results that it possible can. But, it also calls into question some of the older practices of heavily bombarding Google with only one particular keyword. Today, due to the switch to a semantic search, something called Latent Semantic Indexing (LSI) is now more commonplace. This is just a fancy term for similar search keywords. So, if you're searching for a keyword such as "Best Diet Plans," you might find results with keywords optimized for "Top Weight Loss Programs." Google's LSI engine has become more powerful recently, and it weighs multiple factors to help determine the most similar search terms. This way, even if a page is optimized for a keyword that doesn't exactly match the search term, it may come up at the top of Google's SERPs as long as it adheres to the three spectrums of trust.

I know that all of this may sound confusing to you, but as we delve deeper into an understanding of just how this works, you'll get a better sense for just how to approach your SEO work. You see, Google is stretching itself beyond the boundaries of being locked into that one particular keyword. It wants a page that is not only optimized for a certain keyword, but is done so very naturally. That's why LSI is going to be so important in your SEO career. When you properly utilize LSI, you'll not only optimize the page for a particular keyword, but you'll use LSI keywords within the content in order to make it more appealing to Google's algorithms. And, the better you can understand the nature of this new semantic search engine, the more likely you'll be to come up at the top of search results for any given search term.

But, keep in mind that the three spectrums of trust must always be fulfilled. No matter what approach you take in your SEO work, you have to fulfill the three spectrums of trust. When you can do that, and do it in a very high quality way, you'll be sure to rank at the top of Google's SERPs. But, if you ignore the three spectrums of trust, and try to implement a purely low-quality approach that might include content farming and link farming, you'll be far less likely to rank high. This is why Websites like Mashable.com,   TechCrunch.com,   and HuffingtonPost.com continue to get high ranks and high traffic on Google. They consistently provide high-quality content that provides value to those searching out information on the Web. And, as time goes on, and Google notices a particular site putting out more and more quality content, it will continue to rise in its SERPs.

Furthermore, as you put out quality content, and your backlog of articles that provide a lot of value adds up, your newer content will rank higher, faster. That's because as time goes on, the PageRank of your Website will continue to increase. When this happens, Google will also begin spidering your domain much more often. For example, a PageRank 4 Website will be crawled at least once a day, whereas a PageRank 1 Website may be crawled only once a month or once every few months. Once Google knows that a particular site is putting out quality content, it will begin spidering that domain automatically on a more consistent periodic basis. Otherwise, you'll need to ping Google to visit the site each time you release content, which can become a very tedious thing to have to do each time.

So, whatever tactics you do end up employing when conducting your SEO work, keep the notion of always providing value at all times. If at any moment you think about skimping on your content, or providing anything short of something excellent, then you'll merely get SERP results that reflect that. Take the time to do the proper research into whatever it is that you set out to write about. Then, write a very thorough, well-researched article about that topic, and ensure it provides an incredible amount of value. Anytime someone can walk away from your blog post or Website content having learned something that was of a great deal of value, the more likely you're going to be to get into Google's good graces. So, be thorough, be accurate, and consistently deliver high-quality content every time you set out to build out a blog post or article on the Web.

BLACK-HAT SEO

Black-Hat SEO is what brought Google to the brink of a digital war in the first place. Yes, it sounds very dramatic, but it's true. Google threw its might and resources behind the effort to ensure that the relevancy was kept in tact, because without relevancy, Google really has no core business. All of its various services are built on the foundation of relevancy. People know that if they head to a Google search box, through whatever means available to them, that the results will be accurate and relevant. That's how its business was founded, and that's how its business will always be. So, along came this group of Black-Hat SEO specialists who began poking and prodding the Web, decreasing its relevancy. How did they do it? Well, they essentially spammed Google. They blasted thousands of links in various different formats to inorganically increase the search relevancy of a particular low-quality domain or piece of content.

So, what exactly did these Black-Hat SEMs do? Well, a

variety of techniques were implemented in order to manipulate search results. Namely, those techniques are as follows:

- **Keyword Stuffing** – Keyword stuffing can occur in two areas. The one area is within the META keyword tag, which is now obsolete. The other is within the content of the Webpage itself. Keyword stuffing is specifically what it sounds like: overcrowding one or very similar keywords in an effort to get Google to notice and increase the relevancy of that particular Webpage. A common practice some years back, keyword stuffing is something that's still implemented by SEMs unbeknownst to the fact that it will do more harm than good for the Webpage. This is an easy way to get a particular link Sandboxed. Stay away from keyword stuffing.

- **Doorway Pages** – A doorway page is a Webpage that's designed to look different to search engines than it is to real human eyes. So, how is this achieved? Well, several methods can be implemented to create doorway pages. One such method is to use sneaky redirects to send human visitors to different pages than search engines. How is this possible? It's a simple form of light programming to determine whether the visitor is a search engine spider or a human visitor. But, regardless of the methods, it shouldn't be done. It will only harm your Webpage in the long term and potentially have the site Sandboxed by Google.

- **Invisible Text** – Another popular method the Black-Hat SEOs used in the past was invisible text. This can be achieved with simple CSS coding or by changing the color of the text to the same color as the background. The invisible text would allow SEMs to stuff keywords at their heart's desire without cluttering the page to human eyes. But the search engines would find that text. However, today, engaging in this practice will easily get you Sandboxed. So, always stay away from these kinds of manipulative practices or you'll find yourself being penalized by Google.

- **Link Farming** – Link farming is a practice that had become very common amongst the Black-Hat SEO world. When you farm for links, you essentially go out there and create hundreds, if not thousands, of links back to your content through the usage of automatic-link-creation software. This type of practice – namely when creating low-quality links – is a very precarious one to engage in. This is especially true when you don't know precisely what you're doing. Don't engage in link farming of low-quality links unless you know precisely what you're doing. You could easily end up in the Google Sandbox if you do so.

- **Content Farming** – This practice was common for some time, but Google cracked down on this as well. Of course, today this is considered a Black-Hat SEO technique and it involves employing a vast number of freelancers to specifically develop content in order to target search engine algorithms. This content was generally low-quality content that was merely designed to help a site rank higher, faster. With the introduction of the Google Panda and the Google Penguin, this practice is generally not employed anymore. A high-quality approach is now necessary when sculpting or creating any content for the Web.

Many people want to learn about Black-Hat SEO techniques because they think that Black-Hat SEO is going to help them to cheat the search engines and move up the rankings quicker. Now, the way that Google has designed its algorithms is that you won't be able to determine final rank of a search listing right away. When something like Black-Hat SEO is applied to a particular link or Webpage, it may at first move up the listings, but later will fall back down again. That's because Google doesn't want people to know what works and what doesn't immediately. It will move the listings around the SERP in an effort to create some confusion. That's why, at first, it may seem like the Black-Hat SEO techniques are working, but later when the listing falls again, it will be clear that they don't work.

Now, it's important to note that Black-Hat SEO techniques are frowned upon, but it's also going to be important to understand the distinction about what it is regarding these techniques that Google finds so invasive. In essence, Google is trying to limit the effort of individuals who are trying to unnaturally move certain listings around on the Web. However, this also has a lot to do with the underlying Webpage and content. When the content is incredibly high in quality, certain Black-Hat SEO techniques applied in an organic fashion will in effect help that listing more than it will hinder it. Of course, this should only be left to Advanced SEMs, but it's an important distinction to make here. Always keep in mind that content is king, and that high-quality content is going to rule the Web.

You can look at the underlying content almost akin to the foundation of a building. When the foundation is solid, it can support the structure above. But, when the foundation is weak, the structure will collapse. Things like content farming, link farming, and other Black-Hat SEO techniques area going to get Webpages banned from the same search listings that they are targeting. So, extreme caution must be used here. Again, if you don't know what you're doing, you could severely damage the search visibility of your domain name for years to come. If you do happen to end up in the Google Sandbox, then there are ways to crawl out, but the amount of effort it will take will be enormous. It's better to avoid the Sandbox and other Google penalties by trying to adhere as closely to the rules as possible. Always think natural and organic in your mind.

If you're engaging in an SEO practice that isn't natural and organic, then it's not going to get you very far. Try to be sensitive to the fact that, although you might want to employ certain tactics to move you up the search rankings quicker, in the long run it's not going to be worth your while. Take the time and the effort to truly employ a natural and organic approach. Yes, there are ways to bend the rules these days, and you might even get away with it, but it may not be worth it. You can quickly be penalized by crossing that invisible threshold that Google has established. But, by staying in Google's good graces, you can move up the search rankings slowly but steadily. We'll go into what this is going to take moving ahead, but for now, it's important to remember to adhere as closely to the rules as possible.

WHITE-HAT SEO

Today, the best approach that you can take when building out content and optimizing it for Google's search engine algorithms, is to employ White-Hat SEO techniques. But what is White-Hat SEO exactly? Well, it's the usage of methods and techniques pursuant to Google's Webmaster Guidelines. This means that they must comply with what Google is expecting from the Web. The closer that you comply with Google's expectations, the more likely you're going to be able to rank higher, faster.

So, what's it going to take to do just that?

Well, White-Hat SEO is built on a foundation of trust, as it's the basis for any successful SEO campaign today. This isn't to say that a combination of some other techniques won't work, but rather that White-Hat SEO must be the primary basis for any successful campaign. So, with that being said, it's important to explore just what White-Hat SEO techniques are and how they work. Once you have a better understanding of the techniques, we'll visit some strategies for implementing these techniques on new and existing sites. Now, where do we begin?

The Website Fold

To start, it's important to understand some terminology as it relates to Webpages themselves. One important term is the *Website Fold*. The Website Fold is the section of the page that can be seen when first visiting a Webpage. The Website Fold is the section that doesn't require scrolling to be seen upon first arrival at the URL. Everything above that section is considered to be *above the fold*, and everything below that section will be *below the fold*. This is an important distinction to understand because beginning with Google's Panda algorithm update, Google really concentrated on the user's experience, and the Website Fold played a major role in that. When users can't get the information that they're looking for relatively quickly, the user experience is diminished.

For this reason, the Website Fold is important to consider when designing any content or creating any Webpage for that matter. When an individual has to sift past a variety of ads just to get to what they're searching for, the user experience is diminished in Google's eyes. Google wants you to be able to find the information that you're after quickly and effectively. It doesn't want you to have to scroll and sift through Website ads and tremendous amounts of unrelated content. So, it's important to keep the relevant and important information as it pertains to the article or Webpage, above the fold. Crowding a page with too many ads, images, or irrelevant information at the top will push the important content further down the page, and in turn, it will decrease your rankings on SERPs. So, what information are we really talking about then? What has to stay above the fold, and what has to stay below it?

Well, we'll get to more of the specifics when we discuss how content is crafted, but it's important to understand that on any given Webpage, the top-matter must be light. Having large images, or excessively slow-loading menu bars, are going to diminish the user's experience. As you know yourself from searching the Web, when the user experience is diminished, you're less likely to try to sift through the milieu to find what you're looking for. Google knows how quickly Web surfers can get frustrated, so it wants to ensure a clean and relevant search experience for everyone. Now, knowing that this is the case, you have to be highly sensitive to where the information appears on the page. Try to not to clutter the area that's above the fold and ensure that the information in the article appears clearly at the top. This will also include things like the title of the article, relevant heading tags, and keywords as well.

Okay, so you might understand what the Website Fold is, but what are its exact dimensions? What does it mean to have your content above the fold, really? How many pixels does it account for? Well, you must understand that this has a lot to do with average pixel screen sizes. And, since technology is evolving so quickly, this is going to be different at any given moment in time. However, on average, the Website Fold lives somewhere in the 600 pixels to 800 pixels range from the top of the screen. The bulk of the important content should live there and the blog or Webpage's top-matter should be light and condensed. Now, this isn't to say that as things evolve with mobile and wearable computing, that Google won't change some of these rules. But, it's safe to assume that, no matter what date or time we're in, that relevant data should appear as close to the top of the screen as possible. Google simply doesn't want one of its users to have to sift through so many pixels to find the content that he or she is after.

White-Hat SEO Guidelines

The Website Fold is an important distinction, but it isn't the be-all and end-all of Google's rules for a clean White-Hat SEO approach. So, what else is involved? Well, according to Google's Webmaster Guidelines, there are three components involved:

- **Design and Content Guidelines** – Google's design and content guidelines relate to the overall appearance of the site itself and to its functionality. These are aesthetic guidelines but they also include functional ones as well. Most of these guidelines are the basis for the Google Panda algorithm update, and it's important that you adhere to them. Google is merely trying to ensure a rich user experience, allowing a visitor to your site to easily navigate around and find what he or she is looking for quickly.

  o Site hierarchy and text links – Google wants to ensure that the Website has a clear hierarchy and is easy navigable. You must be able to get to any point in the site from any of the other static pages. When designing a site, it's important to keep the site hierarchy in mind. If the site is a blog, then ensure that the menu items allow a user to easily navigate between the sections of the blog to quickly find the information that they're looking for.

o Offer a site map to users – A site map is critical for Google and users. It wants to ensure that not only a search engine be able to find what its looking for quickly, but also users as well. In fact, it's more concerned with how easily users are able to navigate a site than a search engine is. Create a site map, and if there are many pages, break the site map out into multiple pages.

o Reasonable number of links – This rule is both an aesthetic one and a functional one as well. Any time there's an overcrowding of links, Google is sure to take notice. This is especially true when the content is very thin. But, regardless of just how much content is on the page, never overcrowd the page with links out to other sites. This was something common in the content and link farming days, which were the targets of the Google Panda and Google Penguin algorithm updates. Keep the links to a minimum and the content to a very high standard.

o Information-rich content – Google wants to ensure that the content you're providing is information-rich. What does this mean? Well, as previously stated, you must be adding a great deal of value, and it must be unique and engaging. Spend the time to write well-researched articles that help answer questions in the most proficient and well thought out way possible. Never skimp on providing information-rich content. Always think value. Always.

o Keyword-driven content – Google wants to ensure that the Webpage has a purpose, and that the purpose is keyword-driven. Google wants to be able to understand just what the page is about. When the page has no general purpose, Google loses interest and the page loses rank. And, if you're writing a Webpage or article about one particular question or topic, don't veer far off that topic. Stay on the topic and ensure that all of the information and content is relevant to that topic. Don't try to clutter the Webpage with excessive keywords that don't properly pertain to the overall topic of the page.

o Text links as opposed to images – Google can't read images; at least not today, it can't. So, it wants you to use text links as opposed to images wherever possible. Years ago, it was much more difficult to make text appear and aligned like images. But today, with the use of CSS, all that has changed. Try to keep to an all-text and CSS approach if you can, and keep the graphics to a bare minimum while focusing on the content instead. And, when images are used, make sure that they are properly labeled with Image <ALT> tags so that Google can distinguish their purpose.

o Usage of <TITLE> and <ALT> attributes – The <TITLE> tag relates to the Website's header, and it provides the descriptive outline for what the page is about. The <TITLE> tag is also the same tag that's used by Google to provide the title of your page on its SERPs. Ensure that you properly utilize the <TITLE> tag of your page by placing the keyword-rich title there that accurately depicts what the page is about. And, again, when using images on your Webpage, always ensure that <ALT> attributes are used to describe them. Usage of the page's primary keyword in an <ALT> tag is also highly recommended.

o Check for broken links – No one likes broken links, especially Google. If you're creating a Webpage, no matter what it's about, always go back and ensure the accuracy of the links. Do all of the links work? Do all of the links point to valid pages on the Internet? If not, go back and fix them. Google will check your pages for accuracy in broken links. Always ensure that you have a 100% working links ratio to not lose the potential for ranking.

o URL rules for dynamic pages – Whether you're familiar with dynamic pages or not, it's important to keep in mind that Google wants to find the primary keyword in the page's URL or something that's semantically similar to it. Furthermore, when using Web programming such as PHP, more than one variable after the URL won't be indexed (i.e. after the question mark in a PHP-driven URL). Keep the parameters short if you must have them in the URL, since static pages are crawled much more efficiently than dynamic ones are.

o Image rules – Google can't read images. It can't decipher text inside images or other relevant information; at least not at this moment in time. For that reason, you have to be as descriptive as possible with your images. Rather than using a name like IMG12345.jpg, try to name the image with the primary keyword of the page. If the page is about "iPhone 7 Rumors," give the main image a title like iphone-7-rumors-graphic.jpg. This is much more descriptive and informative than a random image name. Furthermore, use the image <ALT> attribute to add further clarification with the keyword. Also, do not attempt to stuff keywords into the image <ALT> attribute, as it will only hurt you as opposed to helping you.

▪ Image quality – Remember to always keep in mind that Google wants browsers to have a rich user experience. Ensure that the quality of your photos is high and that they relevantly pertain to the context of the Webpage that they're on. Google is much more likely to like a page with high-quality photos than one with low-quality photos. Stay away from using blurry or obscure photos that don't pertain to the content. Furthermore, stay away from poaching other images from Websites where possible. Try to keep your content and your images as original as possible. If you must use images found on other sites, be sure to properly label and name them.

- Image Dimensions – Make sure that you always provide a height and a width in pixels for your images. This is achieved by using the height and width attributes within the image tag itself.

- Image Location – Google knows that most users will not scroll to the bottom of the Webpage, so it's important to keep your primary image for the Webpage as close to the top as possible.

o <u>Video rules</u> – Google is constantly improving its search algorithms to encompass a wide variety of searchable data, which includes videos. Videos are a great way to help increase the relevance of a Webpage, but they also must be properly presented and identified to the Google search engine. Google recommends using schema.org for marking up video information on a site.

- **Technical Guidelines** – These guidelines relate more to the technical aspects – namely the coding – of a site or Webpage. These guidelines are important because Google places some weight on the browsability, discoverability, and overall cross-browser experience of any given Webpage. If it feels like a Webpage falls short, so will its rankings. If you're not in-the-know from a coding standpoint, then it's important to find a professional who can help assist in this area.

  o <u>Limit usage of JavaScript, Flash, and DHTML</u> – In an effort to keep load time and cross-browser compatibility at efficient levels, Google discourages the usage of Flash, JavaScript, and DHTML. For the most part, all of this can be achieved today with dynamic HTML markup and CSS, so it's best that you stay away from anything that's going to slow the load time of a Webpage.

o   Handling Session IDs – Session IDs are used very commonly to track the behavior of visitors to sites. These could include things like Website Cookies and Login Sessions. If your site is using sessions, ensure that WebCrawlers will be able to still access the pertinent pages on the site for indexing purposes. It's important that a search engine spider such as Google's be able to crawl without the usage of sessions.

o   HTTP Header support – It's important to ensure that the web server that you're using supports the If-Modified-Since HTTP Header. This allows Google to know whether a Webpage was updated since it last visited the page. This will save bandwidth and overhead in the instance where information was not updated on a particular page since the WebCrawler's last visit.

o   Using robots.txt – This is going to be an important part of the process in SEO. You must ensure that you generate a robots.txt so that unintended pages aren't crawled. You can use robots.txt to tell search engine spiders like Google's to only crawl certain pages or directories.

o   Over-usage of ads – Google doesn't want to see a high ad-to-content ratio. Rather, it wants it to be the other way around. Make sure that your page isn't filled with too many ads. Even if you have many high-quality posts, limit the ads to a reasonable number. Google knows that no user wants to sift through endless amounts of ads, even if the ads are non-invasive and off to the side of the Webpage.

o Crawlable pages with CMS systems – If you're using a CMS system to create your Webpages, it's important that the pages be crawlable. Some CMS systems will create pages and links that search engines can't crawl. Always ensure that all of your pages are properly crawlable and accessible to search engines for the highest-quality browsing experience possible.

o Cross-browser compatibility – Whether it's Internet Explorer, Safari, Firefox, Chrome, or any other browser, always ensure that your pages properly appear across all platforms. You could easily lose search rankings based on Google's algorithms if your pages don't look and behave consistently across browsers. Test and re-test using popular available tools for cross-browser compatibility checks. If you're using Wordpress or other blogging platforms, you'll have less to worry about unless you've created a custom theme.

o Optimization of load-times – Don't overload your pages with heave and slow-loading graphics. This should already be clear to you as it diminishes the user's browser experience. Just imagine yourself when you have to sit through and wait for a slow-loading site to finally load all of its components. Keep the images to a minimum level.

- **Quality Guidelines** – The quality guidelines of a Website have as much to do with Black-Hat SEO as they do with White-Hat SEO. You must adhere to these basic principles and specific practices in order to stay in Google's good graces. By now, you should understand that Google is looking for high-quality content that's engaging and provides value. But you must pay attention to all the other details of aesthetics and functionality as well.

    o Basic Principles

        ▪ Pages designed for users not search engines

        ▪ Avoiding deception

        ▪ Avoiding search-engine-optimization tricks

        ▪ Creating unique content that's engaging and adds value

o Specific Practices

- Avoid automatically generated content

- Don't participate in link schemes

- Don't engage in content cloaking

- Don't engage in sneaky redirects

- Don't hide text or links

- Don't create doorway pages

- Don't scrape content

- Don't participate in affiliate programs without adding a lot of value

- Don't add irrelevant keywords

- Don't create pages with malicious behavior (i.e. phishing, Trojans, malware, viruses, etc.)

- Don't abuse rich-snippet markup

- Don't send automated queries to Google

- Monitor your site for hacking

- Prevent and remove user-generated spam from your site

GRAY-HAT SEO

Now that you have a basic understanding of the difference between Black-Hat SEO and White-Hat SEO, we can discuss something called Gray-Hat SEO. So, what is Gray-Hat SEO? It's the mixture of a very limited selection of Black-Hat SEO techniques in a White-Hat SEO strategy. Now, the premise here has to be that the underlying content is of high quality, is engaging, and provides value. But, all the other guidelines must be adhered to as well. Now, this mainly refers to the utilization of some automated systems on the Web to help speed things along, but it must be done in an organic nature.

So, what do I mean by this?

Well, in some studies that we've conducted here internally, we've concluded that some farming of links that are IP-diverse will in fact help a good solid piece of content. It must be done in a very organic nature, however. So, how is this done? Well, remember the three spectrums of trust? There's trust in age, content, and authority. The former two are relatively straightforward. It's easy to understand that older domain names are going to be trusted more than newer ones, and that excellent content is going to rank higher than sub-par content. But it's the trust in authority that's the variable here.

So, let's look at what I mean by this. First, we know that Google is looking for a very diverse set of backlinks that are coming back to a Website. It wants a wide variety of links that are from authority sites and non-authority sites. Google is also looking for a diverse set of keywords that are linking back as well. As part of its algorithm, it knows that if all of a sudden thousands of backlinks are created to a site in a very short period of time, all with the same keyword, that something fishy is going on. What it wants to see are not only specific keywords that are relevant to the Webpage, but also generic ones as well. That's because Google knows that generic keywords containing links to good content will pop up across the Web. This doesn't just mean on social media sites, but also in blog comments, and forum posts as well.

So, what is a Gray-Hat SEO approach? Well, this is going to involve link farming and sculpting in a way that's natural and organic. However, this is only recommended once you've gotten your bearings and you've learned the ins-and-outs of the SEO world. And, it's something we'll discuss further in subsequent courses. However, as an overall view, it's important to understand that once you've created a high-quality site with content that's engaging and adds value, then you can go on to engaging in these more advanced link-building efforts. This is going to be one of the most time-intensive parts of your SEO work. You'll come to find that building and creating links throughout the Web is going to take a sincere amount of effort on your part. But there are ways to expedite the process, and that's where the Gray-Hat SEO approach comes into play.

Now, again, I'll need to throw up some caution signs here because when you do embark upon a Gray-Hat SEO road, you're risking the chance of being penalized by Google if you don't tread with caution. That's why, if you're new to SEO, you should merely stick with a fully White-Hat SEO approach until you get the hang of things. The Gray-Hat SEO method would only be recommended for intermediate to advanced SEMs who have some experience behind their belts and are ready to tackle more complex SEO campaigns. However, it's not all smoke and mirrors here. These aren't ninja secrets that exist out there that only a select few know about or know how to implement. In fact, these resources are available to everyone out there on the Web that knows just how to implement them.

So, what does this involve? Well, Gray-Hat SEO is primarily based upon link building, because that's a core component of SEO. Sure, you have to have a quality site that plays by the rules along with quality content. But, once you have the fundamentals in place, then it's time to get out there and start building links. In the subsequent SEO University course entitled, *SEO Strategies and Tactics*, you'll learn just how to utilize a slew of services that exist on the Web to build both high-quality and low-quality links to your content that's very IP-diverse and keyword-diverse as well. For now, we'll be covering all the other fundamental principles involved with researching keywords, crafting content, and engaging in SEO work that will help you build a better understanding of how things work. In the subsequent course, you'll be exposed to more of the advanced strategies and tactics for ranking today.

4

KEYWORD RESEARCH

Much of your work in the field of SEO is going to be keyword-centric. As you'll come to find, you'll be building your content designed around a specific primary keyword. Why is that? Well, as we've already seen, Google wants to quickly and accurately be able to determine just what a piece of content is about. It doesn't want to have to guess. It bases this on the understanding that any good piece of high-quality content will be specifically targeted at one precise topic, question, or area of interest. So, it's going to be looking very carefully at some very exact criteria to help determine what the page is about. For this reason, it's important that you work on gearing your content and sculpting it towards a specific purpose.

However, firstly, it's important to look at just what a keyword is. Some people are under the misconception that a keyword is a single word. It's not. A keyword can be a word, group of words, or a phrase that's used to help Google determine what the Webpage's content is about.

Of course, a keyword can be just a single word, but those keywords would be next to impossible to compete over. Plus, there's no specificity there. If you try to search for the term "Help" on Google, you most likely won't find the type of help that you're looking for. However, if you search using a keyword such as "Help me find a doctor nearby," you might find something more closely depicting your search. You see Google wants to help you find the answer to your questions as quickly and efficiently as possible. Part of that, is that it wants you to provide as much information as possible.

You're most likely versed in searching on Google already, so you've more than likely done thousands if not tens of thousands of searches. You know that you're more likely to find what you're looking for when you provide more details. For example, rather than searching for "Restaurants in San Francisco," you know that you'll get a better result if you search a term like "Best Italian Restaurants in San Francisco." When you search the latter term, you're going to get a list of results that will more likely help you to accurately find the type of food you're looking for. So, just as if you were searching for something yourself on the Web, when you work to determine what keyword you want to optimize for, you have to consider these things. Think about what you would search for if you were looking for your products or services on the Web. What term would you likely use?

And, as we discussed before, Google doesn't like to find irrelevant content or superfluous keywords. Although it wants you to provide enough description to find what you're looking for, in the case of a Webpage, it doesn't want it to supply keywords that don't apply to the content. This is also known as keyword stuffing. In some of the rules that you've seen thus far, you may have noted that Google doesn't like irrelevant keywords that don't pertain to the piece of content. For that reason, every part of a

Webpage or blog post must be specifically targeted towards that primary keyword. So, keep this in mind whenever you approach any Webpage content-building project or article post. Make sure that your content is very specific and targeted. If you don't know what you're going to write about, then you must determine that first before doing anything else.

So, your content must not only be high-quality content that's engaging and provides value, but it must also be keyword-driven content. Now that you understand the importance of this, it's time to understand just how to research those keywords in order to create a piece of content that's not only targeted, but also rankable as well. Because, it's better to place on the first page for a keyword that will get you little traffic, than to be on a higher page for a more popular keyword search and get virtually no traffic. So, the goal is to be able to rank on Google's SERPs and begin to drive at least some free organic traffic to your Website. So, where do we begin?

To begin researching keywords, we'll actually be using a tool that's provided by the search giant itself, entitled "Keyword Planner." This keyword planner is designed for advertisers who utilize Google's Adwords system in order to place ads that appear within its network of sites. When you get to the Keyword Planner page, it will look like the proceeding image.

Keyword Planner
Plan your next search campaign

What would you like to do?

  ▸ Search for new keyword and ad group ideas

  ▸ Get search volume for a list of keywords or group them into ad groups

  ▸ Get traffic estimates for a list of keywords

  ▸ Multiply keyword lists to get new keyword ideas

Keyword Planner Tips

Building a Display campaign? Try Display Planner

How to use Keyword Planner

Learn how Keyword Planner is different from Keyword Tool

On the page, there will be four separate options:

- Search for new keyword and ad group ideas

- Get search volume for a list of keywords or group them into ad groups

- Get traffic estimates for a list of keywords

- Multiply keyword lists to get new keyword ideas

To get started, we'll search for the term that we're looking for using the "Search for new keyword and ad group ideas" link. When we use that link, we'll receive a slew of options that will allow you to determine the best keyword as your primary keyword. You can type in ideas, business type, industry type, a question, or any word or phrase into this box, and you'll get back ideas for keywords you can use. The best part about this system is that, not only does Google provide you with keyword ideas, but it also tells you just how many people are searching for that keyword every month and how competitive the search is. So, if you find a good keyword, but you notice that it has high competition, then you'll know to stay away from that particular keyword until you've built lots of trust with

Google across all three spectrums.

This Keyword Planner Tool is going to be one of the most important tools that you're going to use in your SEO career, so it's important to get to know it well. When you conduct your search for keywords, the two most important columns are going to be the "Average Monthly Searches" column and the "Competition" column. Always pay careful attention to those two columns as the keyword that you select should be heavily influenced by how competitive that search term is and how many people are searching for it every month. Furthermore, if you're just starting out in SEO, or if you have a brand new domain name with little to no trust in age, then you should go after Low Competition Keywords. There's also a nominal competition keyword, which is indicated by a hyphen "-" in the competition column. Remember, it's better to show up at the top of results for a minimal amount of monthly searches, than nowhere at all for a high volume of monthly searches.

So, as an example, when you conduct a search for the keyword, "how to beat procrastination," you're able to select between two separate tabs: the "Ad group ideas," and the "Keyword ideas." When you select the "Keyword ideas" tab, you'll get a list of keywords that would apply to this type of content. And, when you click on the "Competition" heading, you'll be able to order the results from low to high competition. This way, you can see all of the keyword ideas that will be easy to compete for, first. So, this is going to be the way you're going to select your primary keyword. It's important to choose one main keyword here, then some secondary ones as well. Why choose secondary keywords? That's because although Google doesn't want to see irrelevant keywords on a page, it does like to see some relevant keywords. Find similar keywords that are relevant to the primary keyword and jot those down. Make sure that the competition is low for them all unless you have some SEO experience behind your belt. You won't be able to successfully compete for medium or high-competition keywords at first until you build up your levels of trust with Google.

BRAINSTORMING KEYWORDS

Sometimes, it's harder than we may think to brainstorm and come up with a set of keywords that we can use to optimize our pages with. It's important to spend the right amount of time during this step of the process because it's going to be the basis for your SEO work. Finding the right keywords from the beginning is going to be crucial to your chances of ranking high, fast. Take the time to jot down as much information as you possibly can about the industry that you're in, the subject matter, competitors, customer types, customer needs, and so on, that you can think of. Brainstorm on a sheet of paper and come up with as many ideas as possible before you start compare and analyze those keywords with Google's Keyword Planner.

Once you have a set of ideas for keywords, especially if you have multiple ideas, by using the Keyword Planner, you can better determine which keyword would be the most efficient usage of your time. If you're able to find good keywords with low competition but high search volume, then that's what you're looking for. Although they may be rare, by lengthening the keywords, you'll be more likely to find them. This would be called a *long-tail keyword*. A long-tail keyword is different from a short-tail keyword in that it will have five or more words in it. This could also be considered as questions or longer phrases that are more specific. For example, rather than writing an article or a blog post on "How to lose weight," which will be difficult to rank for, try your hand at a keyword like "How to lose weight in 30 days without exercise."

Can you see how the long-tail keyword would be easier to rank for? That's because less people are going to search for a term that's longer than they will for one that's shorter. Still, if your Website is brand new and it has very little in the way of established trust from Google across the three spectrums, it's going to be considerably easier to rank for a long-tail keyword. So, in the beginning, you should try to focus your efforts on the long-tail keywords as opposed to the short-tail keywords. You can certainly throw some short-tail keywords in the mix there, but it's much better to select a primary keyword that's a long-tail keyword than one that's a short-tail keyword.

LSI KEYWORDS

In an early chapter, I alluded to something called LSI, or latent semantic indexing. This technology uses a mathematical method called singular value decomposition (SVD) to find patterns in the relationships of words and phrases in a given text. LSI is also a technology that is now being heavily relied upon by Google to determine a similar keyword for a search term that better meets its three spectrums of trust. So, in an example, let's say we did a search for "Best way to lose weight fast." In this type of a search, we might not have that specific keyword match come up in the first few listings, especially if no one has taken the time to optimize for that exact keyword that meets the three spectrums of trust. However, in its place, Google will retrieve closely resembling keywords from Websites that do meet its three spectrums of trust.

In this example, when searching for "Best way to lose

weight fast," the first result from Google is the keyword "Best way to lose weight in a week," from Cosmopolitan.com. Cosmopolitan.com is a trusted Website on Google, and in fact, the page that ranks at the top of Google's search results has a PageRank of 5, which is incredibly high. The second search result, from Health.com, has a PageRank of 6. So, why does a PageRank 5 Webpage rank higher than a PageRank 6 Webpage? Well, it's based on the three components of trust. While both Websites were registered towards the end of 1998, the first Website has 3,242 Tweets to its page, whereas the second one only has 26 Tweets. Both Websites have a closely similar amount of shares on Facebook – 4,400 for the first listing, and 4,900 for the second listing. However, the strong social signals here of the 3,242 Tweets on the first listing versus the 26 Tweets on the second listing, help it to rank higher. In the proceeding image, you'll see this quantified using the SEO Quake Toolbar.

But what's the SEO Quake Toolbar? Well, the SEO Quake Toolbar is either a plugin or an extension for a browser that allows you to conduct searches with x-ray lenses. What do I mean by this? Well, when you install the SEO Quake Toolbar, you get to see what Google sees about each particular listing. This helps you to better assess just what it's going to take to compete for any given keyword search. So, when used in conjunction with the Keyword Planner Tool from Google, it allows you to have full information about any given search term. This information is important as it allows you to understand just how difficult it's going to be to rank. You'll understand just how this works as you analyze more and more search data. The more times you look at the levels of competition using the Keyword Planner Tool, in conjunction with data collected using the SEO Quake Toolbar, the better you'll become at planning your keywords.

Can you also notice the differentiation in LSI keywords in the image here? You'll see that the titles for the top four search listings for "Best way to lose weight fast" are as follows:

- The Best Way to Lose Weight in a Week

- 16 Ways to Lose Weight Fast

- 50 Easy Ways to Lose Weight

- How to Lose Weight Fast and Safely

As you'll notice, none of these top four listings are an exact match to the keyword that we searched for. In fact, none of the first page's search results exactly match that search term. These are the LSI variations of that search term. Google is finding listings that best match the query from Websites that fulfill its three spectrums of trust. Now, You'll notice in the preceding image that a small toolbar from SEO Quake shows up below each listing. This is how you'll use SEO Quake to see just how Google is seeing those listings. This helps you to determine just how well those listings are fulfilling two of the three spectrums of trust: age and authority. The age of the domain is listed under each listing along with several trust through authority components such as: number of links to the domain, number of Tweets, number of Facebook Shares, number of Google Plus Ones and so on.

I know that LSI might sound like a confusing term to you or even very complicated, but it's not really. LSI is just another way to look at a search term. Just like the example of "Best Way to Lose Weight Fast," brought up something like "50 Easy Ways to Lose Weight," other LSI keywords are going to exist. So, how do you actually determine what an LSI keyword is going to be? And, what impact is this going to have on your optimization efforts? Well, selecting LSI keywords shouldn't be too difficult because, when you're using the Google Keyword Planner, most of the suggestions will be LSI variations of the original keyword entered in. However, this isn't to say that it would suggest something like "16 Ways to Lose Weight Fast" when entering in "Best Way to Lose Weight Fast," but those are merely titles for articles based upon content developed.

So, you have to ask yourself some questions at this point to help you determine just what LSI keywords you're going to use. That's because the LSI keywords are going to be integral to your optimization efforts. Not only does Google use LSI when returning results based on page titles on SERPs, but it also uses LSI within content to judge trust through content. Now, most of what we've been looking at here is building trust through authority, but we've yet to look at how to build trust through content. For now, you have to keep in mind that LSI variations for your primary keyword are going to be the secondary relevant keywords that you'll use to optimize your page with. In the coming chapters, we'll go over just how to do this in detail.

5
BUILDING TRUST THROUGH AGE

Now that you've had a brief overview of just what SEO is, we can take the first steps of putting into practice all of the theory. So, as you already know, the three elements of trust that Google is looking for is: trust through age, trust through authority, and trust through content. Let's look at just how we build trust through age. This spectrum of trust is much more difficult to achieve than the other ones, because you can't force trust through age. You either have it or you don't. But, what does this necessarily mean and how does trust through age work?

Well, depending on whom you ask in the industry, opinions will differ on the trust through age spectrum of trust with Google. But, you can look at it like this. When a new business opens it doors, and has yet to gain a track record and trusted reputation over time, people will treat it with suspect. If the owner of that same business tries to walk into a bank to get a new business loan, they'll fail to do so merely on the merits of the business because of its age. Recently launched websites are newcomers to the block, and Google looks at them the same way a bank would look at a new business.

But how new is too new?

Well, websites that aren't aged for at least two years are going to have a harder time being ranked on Google's SERPs. But, this doesn't mean that the domain name must have been registered two years or more ago. It means that Google must have found that Website and indexed it as well. So, if Google didn't find the Website and index it in its indexes, then the aging process couldn't have started. But, if the domain name was indexed two or more years ago, then it's considered aged. Now, how do you get around this? If you'll recall the discussion at the beginning of this book, Google will Sandbox new sites and sites that have misbehaved. So, if the site is new, then its SEO impact will be filtered.

Now, if you have a brand new domain and you're unable to change it, then you're stuck having to build authority over time. In this scenario, SEMs are going to have a much harder time building authority because of Google's Sandbox. However, if you're in a position where you can purchase something called an aged domain, then this would be the ideal route to travel down. Now, it's important to keep in mind that purchasing an aged domain name is not the most White-Hat SEO approach. In fact, it would be considered a Gray-Hat SEO approach. The challenge here is purchasing an aged domain name that not only was indexed in the past two or more years by Google, but that its historical content matches the intended present-day content that you plan to create.

So, how do you purchase an aged domain, and is it that necessary? Well, purchasing an aged domain name is somewhat similar to purchasing a new domain, except with some subtle differences. Firstly, when you purchase an aged domain name, you won't have that domain name transferred to you immediately. When you purchase them through an auction house like GoDaddy Auctions, you'll need to wait several days to upwards of a week or two until the transfer is complete. This is completely dependent upon the auction house and just how long the transfer may take, will depend on them.

Now, it's important to make some distinctions here first. There are some points that are going to be important to understand as far as aged domain names are concerned.

#1 – Historically Indexed Content

Firstly, you must understand that if you're going to purchase an aged domain name, the historically indexed pages of the domain name are going to have to closely match the content that you wish to produce. This means that if you intend on creating a technology blog, don't purchase a domain name that was indexed by Google for healthcare content. This may or may not be considered as Black-Hat SEO by Google, so be wary of the historical content. In order to determine the historical content of any given domain name, simply use the Wayback Machine. The Wayback Machine is an Internet Archive of sorts that can be found at: http://archive.org/web.

When you arrive at the Wayback Machine, you'll be able to enter in any domain name right in the search box. No matter what domain name you enter, you'll receive a historical index, or no index at all. The historical index will be broken down into years and months and will show bar-graph activity during the life of the domain name. Depending on what domain name you key in, either you'll find lots of historical activity, or you'll find none. Now, remember, even though a domain name was registered years ago, if Google never indexed it, then it's not considered an aged domain name. This specific online tool will help you determine whether Google indexed the domain in the past. If it did, then you'll be able to have a glimpse into what the physical pages of the site looked like. When you can look at the pages, you can determine whether the historically indexed content is going to support the future intended content.

So, once you've conducted a search for the domain name in question, look at the historically indexed pages. Click on them to see just what Google saw and indexed in its vast array of data on the Web. If you can find something that's relatively similar to the intended content that you're looking to put out, then it could be a good fit. The other thing that you're going to want to look for here is that the historically indexed data goes back two or more years. And if you can find one that goes back at least five or more years, then that would be even better. Look carefully at the historically indexed pages by clicking on the various areas on the bar graph. As you'll see in the proceeding image from amazon.com, you'll notice just how much historically indexed data there is.

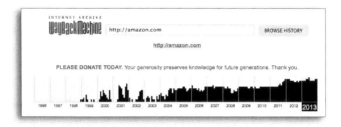

As you can see in the traffic patterns on this page, amazon.com is a very busy domain name. But, more importantly, from this information we can gather what the historically indexed content of amazon.com was. Now, of course, we're not attempting to buy this as an aged domain name, but this should give you an idea of how the process works. When you click on any of the years, you'll be presented with a calendar just below that will show you the dates in the year and links to any pages with historically indexed content that may exist. For amazon.com, the calendar is filled with blue circles and it contains a vast amount of historically indexed Webpages. But, since this process will be necessary to do when researching domain names, it's important that you see just what the Webpages look like.

When we look at amazon.com, historically speaking, we'll find what we would expect to find: the world's biggest electronic retailer and its homepage. Depending on what year you select, you'll see different Webpages presented. This is important when researching an aged domain name to purchase. Depending on what domain names you find available through GoDaddy Auctions, the historically indexed page content is going to help with your decision to purchase that domain name or not. Conduct a careful analysis of the pages to ensure that your content is going to be inline with the historically indexed content. No matter what domain name you select, as long as its aged with congruent content to the type that you intend to produce, then you'll be in good shape to purchase that domain name.

#2 – Sandboxed Domains

One of the pitfalls of searching for aged domain names is potentially coming across and purchasing a domain that has been Sandboxed by Google. As you know, the Google Sandbox is a place where not only brand new domain names go, but also ones that have been misbehaving. Spotting a Sandboxed domain name may be a bit tricky. Without having first-hand knowledge of the domain and its activity, it's going to be difficult to do. But, some indicators can help you make a better judgment call. Firstly, you have to look for domain names that have two or more years of indexed data by Google. The Wayback Machine can help with that. But, in order to spot a Sandboxed domain name, you have to carefully survey the peaks and valleys of the graph.

So, what does a Sandboxed domain name look like?

Well, you might be able to spot a Sandboxed domain name by looking at major drop-offs in traffic. As you can see in the Amazon chart, there is a steady incline in traffic over the years. However, not all domain names look like this. Some show sporadic activity, and some show activity that substantially decreases from one year to the next. But, this could also indicate the fact that the domain name switched hands during that time. If the traffic saw a major decrease, it wouldn't always signify that the domain was Sandboxed. But, in order to see if this happened, just look at the historically indexed content. If the Webpage content changed, and there's a clear indication of new ownership through a differing logo or homepage design, and so on, then that could mean the domain wasn't Sandboxed. If, however, it's clear that that the domain name didn't change hands, then this could indicate that the domain was Sandboxed.

Sound confusing?

I know that it may be a lot to take in, but it's necessary when engaging in this Gray-Hat SEO approach. And, it's important to note here that if you don't feel comfortable with this approach, then you shouldn't go down this path. It isn't for everyone. However, it is a way to expedite the spectrum of trust through age, something that's become very hard to achieve now without having some history with Google. If you purchase an aged domain name, then you might get yourself into good graces with Google as long as you play by all the other rules. Don't try to purchase an aged domain name and build subpart content, then engage in link schemes that generate only low-quality links. Try to play as closely by the rules as possible, even if you do purchase an aged domain name.

The whole point here is that Google is looking for

quality, relevant content. If you can brush past some of the other delimiting factors associated with registering a brand new domain name, then you might make things easier on yourself. Since the road to SEO domination is going to be a long and arduous one, we can use all the help that we can get. Aged domain names can offer you that kind of help, so they're certainly beneficial in helping you get things off the ground. And, now that you know a little bit about how to research aged domain names, you'll probably want to understand the steps that are involved with purchasing one. Once you understand how the entire process works, you can begin conducting searches for aged domain names that may historically match the type of content you're intending on putting out onto the Web.

USING GODADDY AUCTIONS

In order to research and purchase an aged domain name, head over to the GoDaddy Auctions Website. You can find it at the following URL: http://auctions.godaddy.com. Once you get to the screen, which is depicted in the proceeding image, you'll be able to conduct a search for your domain name. To do this, click on the "advanced search" link shown right next to the main search box on the page, indicated by the red arrow.

Once you click on the "advanced search" link, you'll come to a page with a variety of search options as depicted in the proceeding image. You'll want to modify some of the criteria in order to suit your search for the perfect aged domain name. Here's what you'll want to modify:

- <u>Keywords</u> – Change to "Contains" because if not, it will search out only those keywords that exactly match your search. For example, if you were to enter in travel, it would only search for travel.com. If you change this to "Contains," then it will search out all domain names that contain the keyword "travel."

- <u>Attributes</u> – Select the "Buy Now Option" here in order to find domain names that are available for immediate purchase and not just for an auction that you would have to wait for.

- Domain Age – Set the minimum age here that you want to appear. You can use, 2, 3, 4, 5, or any other number. The lower the number, the more results you're likely going to pull.

After you conduct your search for a domain name, you'll get a list of search results with the various options that are available, as depicted in the example in the proceeding image. The keyword used in this particular search was "travel," and as you can see, there are a variety of different search results. And, the best way to find the proper domain name here to purchase is to organize the results by traffic level by clicking the "Traffic" column heading. This will place the highest trafficked Websites at the top of the list.

Once you've found a domain name that you think may work for you, before purchasing, you have to ensure that it's an aged domain. Use the technique described utilizing the Wayback Machine, and do your due diligence on each of the domains listed. Before you purchase anything, ensure that not only is it aged, but also that the historically indexed content is going to match the type and style of content that you intend to create with the domain name. This will give you a severe leg up in the race for trust through age with Google. You may also want to conduct a few Google searches using that domain name to see if you can uncover something that may hurt you moving forward. For example, if that domain name was an ecommerce site or another type of site that developed a bad reputation, you might want to stay away from it.

Once you've zeroed in on the domain name that you want to purchase, go through the purchase process by clicking on the "Buy Now" link for the respective row that the domain name is located in. Once you've purchased the domain name, you'll be able to come back, look at your "Bidding List," and look at the domain names that you've won. This is where you'll find out just how long the transfer process is going to take. It can take from 3 days to

2 weeks or more, so be prepared to wait. However, it's better to wait a short period for an aged domain name, than to not wait at all for a brand new domain name with no trust built with Google. The time spent waiting for the domain name to transfer will be time that you can use to strategize your SEO game plan.

Also, keep in mind that the domain name is going to need to be setup somewhere. Now, I won't be covering the logistics of domain name hosting and setup in this guide, and you should already have some knowledge behind your belt in this area. If you have difficulty with this, GoDaddy has plenty of resources on how to update and change the DNS of your domain name to point to the chosen hosting product that you've selected. Be sure to get setup with an excellent blogging platform that you can then integrate with the domain name. Because, the best type of content is going to be fresh content, so you're going to want to build your Website on a blogging platform such as Wordpress. Take the time to familiarize yourself with a system like Wordpress and follow the guidelines in this course for a White-Hat SEO configuration.

Some of the important things to keep in mind are that

you're going to want to ensure that not only do you develop high-quality content that's engaging and provides value, but also that you create and build a clean site that will be easy to navigate with most of the content above the fold. If you remember our conversation about content above and below the fold, you'll need to keep in mind those points when setting out to design your site. Keep the header design light, and the menu items text-based so that the page is optimized for fast load-time. When you add photos to your posts, add only high-quality photos that are accompanied by high-quality text. What's important here it to pay attention to all the details, and don't skimp anywhere. Google wants to satisfy its customers by displaying the best results at the top of its SERPs, so you're going to have to fight to get to the top.

There's so much competition out there that if you don't ensure you're providing the highest quality content and site possible, you're going to be less likely to rank higher, faster. However, if you do follow along with all the guidelines, and begin to win Google's trust, you'll build up a site that Google will begin to recognize and index far more often. This will help you in building PageRank across the entire site as time goes on and you add more content to the mix. There's so much work to do when you're engaged in SEO and so many SEMs try to take shortcuts with content, but they end up falling short on the SERPs. Don't try to take shortcuts, especially when it comes to the creation of high-quality content. Keep these concepts in mind always when conducting any SEO efforts and, over time, you'll be sure to win the game of rank.

6
BUILDING TRUST THROUGH CONTENT

Now that you understand how to build trust through age, let's look at what it really means to build trust through content. As you've already seen me indicate throughout the pages of this course, trust through content is built by creating excellent high-quality content that's engaging and provides value. But how is this done exactly? Well, we've gone through the keyword research phase, so you should know just how to research the proper long-tail or short-tail keywords for your content by now. However, once you have your keyword, how do you actually create high-quality content that's engaging and provides an exceedingly high amount of value? Well, if you've never written an article or blog post in your life before, you might find this a tad bit more difficult. But, either way, you're going to have your work cut out for you.

When we talk about building trust through content, we're actually referring to something called On-Page SEO, sometimes also referred to as On-Site SEO. Simply put, this is merely the SEO work that goes on directly on the Website or Webpage itself and not away from it. In contrast to this, Off-Page SEO, also referred to as Off-Site SEO, is all the SEO work that goes on away from the Website or Webpage itself. We'll be covering Off-Page SEO in the coming chapter, but for now, we'll be focusing on On-Page SEO. As you'll come to find in your SEO career, On-Page SEO is going to be considerably easier to tackle than Off-Page SEO. Why is that? Because you actually have control of the On-Page SEO elements at work here. It's much more difficult to tackle Off-Page SEO, because you'll be dealing with building authority and rank over time through other trusted sites on the Web. It will take a significant amount more of your time and effort to engage in Off-Page SEO than it will to engage in On-Page SEO.

Now that this distinction is clear, one thing that you really have to keep in mind at this stage is that there is a tremendous amount of competition on the Web. And, if you're a brand new domain name, or even an aged domain name, you're going to have a steep hill to climb. You're going to want to create value that competes with Websites that have been around far longer, have far more trust through authority and domain age than you do. So, it's going to take a tremendous amount of effort on your part to create this content. Knowing all of this, and how much competition there is to rank on Google's SERPs, you really have to take the time to craft excellent content. Don't skimp on this. Write content that anyone would be proud to read. Even if you've never written an article or a blog post in the past before, spend as much time researching and writing this, since you need to create something that's excellent.

Exceed the standards out on the Web. Go beyond the call of duty. That's what it's going to take to build rank.

That's what it's going to take to have Google sit up and take notice of your site. And, when you have excellent content behind your belt, other people will take notice too. Google knows that Websites with excellent content will be shared and linked to far more often than sites that don't. And, it pays attention to these social cues. We'll get into how to build trust through authority in the coming chapter, but for the time being, your focus should be on creating excellent high-quality content that's engaging and provides an exceedingly high amount of value. So, this is what you'll need to do in order to get Google's attention. Make sure you do it and you do it to the best of your abilities.

Now that this point is clear, we have to set about on the journey of crafting excellent high-quality content that's not only engaging and provides exceedingly high value, but that's also keyword-driven. If you'll remember in one of the previous sections where I discussed that Google doesn't want to have to guess what the content is about. Well, Google doesn't want to have to guess. It wants to know immediately what the content is about, and it wants to ensure that the piece of content is very much geared towards the keyword it's targeting. It doesn't want to find irrelevant keywords, an over usage of ads, hidden text or links, and so on. It wants good clean content that it can rank on its SERPs. Don't even think about providing anything less than this; and don't think about providing content that tries to break the rules either.

You'll also want to ensure that you have a good system for creating Website content such as Wordpress. I'll be referencing Wordpress throughout this course, as it's presently the most widely used system for blogging on the Web. So, if you're not familiar with a system like Wordpress, then it's important that you do familiarize yourself with it. Take the time to learn how to utilize Wordpress as it will give you the most out of your SEO experience by allowing you to constantly create high-quality content that's engaging, provides value, and is keyword-driven. You can download a free copy of Wordpress at http://www.wordpress.org, or you can setup Wordpress hosting at any of the major hosting companies such as GoDaddy.com, Hostgator.com, and 1and1.com.

BUILDING KEYWORD-DRIVEN CONTENT

Now that we've laid the groundwork, it's time to get busy constructing content and understanding just how to write good content that's rankable on Google's SERPs. Since we've already been through the keyword-research phase, this is the time to gather your keywords up for inclusion in your article. The one thing that you have to always keep in mind is that you're going to want your article or blog post to always have a very specific purpose in mind. That's why you're going to want to create it geared towards one particular keyword, which will be your primary keyword. You should also collect secondary keywords, which would be considered as your LSI keywords, for inclusion in the article.

Remember, Google wants to see content that's not only high-quality, engaging, delivers value, and is keyword-driven, but also sounds natural and organic. And, the best way to make an article sound natural and organic is to use LSI versions of the primary keyword. This is what Google will be looking for. In the recent Hummingbird update, Google has gone to great lengths in its quest for a fully semantic-driven Web search. This means that it wants to be able to answer your questions to the best of its ability, and a lot of that has to do with LSI. Google wants to understand what you're asking for, and if possible, be able to immediately provide the answer to your question directly at the top of its search results. If it's a simple math question such as addition, division, subtraction, or multiplication, Google provides the answer right at the top of its SERPs.

For example, if you type in "10 times 10" in a Google search bar, you're going to get "100" as an answer along with a calculator to do further calculations. You see Google is trying to answer your question to the best of its ability. It knows that by doing this, it's going to draw in the most customers by being a high-quality search engine that more and more people will turn to in an effort to gain answers to their questions. This is Google's mission. Remember the discussion about relevancy? Well, this is the most relevant way to answer a person's question, by providing it right at the top of search results without having to click through to any further pages.

There are other instances of semantic search on Google as well, such as with conversions between units of measurement. For example, if you wanted to find the equivalent of 100 pounds in kilograms, you could type in something like "100 pounds in kg" and you'll get the answer of "45.3592 kg" along with a calculator to conduct further conversions above the search results. Again, this is in Google's quest to help you find the most relevant answer without having to sift through a variety of page results. Of course, this doesn't apply to answers to lengthy questions that require full-page articles such as "Best Way to Lose Weight Fast," but it does apply to other simpler questions. However, even in the keyword search for "Best Way to Lose Weight Fast" Google uses LSI to give you the most accurate answer that most closely matches your question at the top of its SERPs.

ON-PAGE OPTIMIZATION APPROACH

Now that you understand Google's quest in semantic search, it's time for you to understand how to construct a piece of content that's keyword-driven. Now, I can't assist you with ensuring that the content is high-quality content, engaging, and provides value. That's really up to you to ensure. However, you should abide by some general content-creation guidelines when constructing your high-quality content. Here are the general rules that you should follow:

- Content Length – The content length should be at least 500 to 1000 words in length. Ensure that when you're creating your high-quality content that none of it sounds spammy, forced, or has spelling and grammatical errors. All of these would bring the quality of the content down in Google's eyes, and thus the relevancy, so do your best to ensure that it looks and sounds as perfect as possible.

- Keyword Density – The keyword density relates to the number of times a keyword appears versus the total number of words in the article. Now, this keyword density is going to be calculated by both the primary keyword and the secondary keywords that include LSI variations of the primary keyword. The total keyword density that you're going to reach for this is going to be 2% to 5% so you'll want to have 2 to 5 keywords for every 100 words of your article. So, if you have a 500-word article, then the optimal keyword length is going to be 10 to 25 keywords. And, for a 1000-word article, it's going to be 20 to 50 keywords.

- Keyword in URL – Ensure that the page title contains the primary keyword or an LSI version of it. You can turn on page titles in Wordpress by going to Settings > Permalinks > Post name. This will use the Wordpress title to generate a page name, which can then be edited before publication. Remember the discussion about image names and how Google wants a relevant name to the image? Well, the same rule applies to the page name itself. The more specific the title, and the more it applies overall primary keyword of the content, the better.

- <u>Keyword in Title</u> – Use the primary keyword or an LSI version of it in the page's title, which is generally considered the <H1> tag. You should also use the keyword in at least one <H2> tag and <H3> tag. Furthermore, you should section off your article or post so that it's not just one long piece of content. Google wants content that's easy to read and digestible, and section headings assist in that. Ensure that you break up your article into multiple sections, and use the primary keyword and LSI versions of it in those headings.

- <u>Keywords in Content</u> – Ensure that you use your primary keyword or an LSI variation of it at least once in the first paragraph and once in the last paragraph of the content. Google places special weight on these sections of the content as it further clarifies that this piece of content is about is about your primary keyword. You should also distribute the remainder of your keywords throughout the balance of your content, but ensure that it never sounds forced. Spammy content that just attempts to use a maximum amount of keywords will not win points with Google. Google will consider this keyword stuffing.

- <u>Keyword Styling</u> – Ensure that you style your primary keyword or the LSI variations of it. This means that you should use your keyword at least once in boldface font, once in italics, and once in underlined font. Again, this helps to further clarify and target this piece of content to that keyword. Make sure to distribute your stylized texts throughout the content of the Webpage and don't place them all in one section or paragraph. Overall, try to achieve a good balance of keywords throughout the article, without flooding one particular paragraph or section of it.

- <u>Keyword in Meta Description</u> – If you're unfamiliar with a Webpage's meta description, now's the time to familiarize yourself with it. The page's title is the title tag that you'll see on Google searches when you obtain search results, and the description will actually come from the meta description. Now, if the page doesn't have a meta description, then Google will find a paragraph that will best describe the content itself. But, it's best to go out here and create your own meta description. By default, you currently cannot create a unique meta description for each article posted on Wordpress blogs. But, you can download a plugin such as the <u>Yoast SEO Plugin</u> in order to modify the meta description per article posted on your Wordpress blog.

- <u>Keywords in Images</u> – You have at least one high-quality photo on your blog and you should name it with your keyword or an LSI variation of it. Furthermore, when you upload your photo, you should add an ALT tag with your keyword or the LSI variation of it. This will solidify the purpose of the Webpage or article, since the image will drive home the fact that this is a keyword-driven page and just what that keyword is.

On-Page Optimization

1 Use the primary keyword once in page title <H1> tag, once in an <H2> tag and once in an <H3> tag

2 Use the primary keyword in the first paragraph and in the last paragraph

4 Use the primary keyword **once in bold font**, once *in italics font*, and once in underlined font

6 Use the primary keyword in the Webpage or article's meta description

<H1> How to Stop Smoking Fast </H1>

3 Use the primary keyword in the image ALT tag for the Webpage

5 Use a primary keyword density of 2% to 5% that sounds natural and flows organically

7 Make sure primary keyword shows up in the page title, if you are using Wordpress, turn on permalinks and use the "postname" option

7
BUILDING TRUST THROUGH AUTHORITY

As I made mention to at the opening of the last chapter, building trust through authority is going to be the most difficult part of your SEO work. This is also referred to as Off-Page SEO, since it's all the SEO work done away from the Webpage or Website itself. So, what does it take to actually build trust through authority? How do you go about the process of carefully building up the SEO presence of your Website with search engines like Google? Well, it's going to have to be a fully organic-like approach. What I mean by an organic-like approach is that it can't come across forced. For example, if there were no links existing to your Website, and all of a sudden, thousands of links were created all with similar keywords from low-quality sites, Google will know you're cheating. This is the complete opposite of an organic-like approach.

Also, when I talk about organic-like approach, what I'm really referring to is a Gray-Hat SEO method. Now, to really engage in this method, you have to first take a fully organic approach before you switch over to an organic-like approach. What I mean by this is that you must build real authority over time during the first few months, and then switch to an organic-like approach. Why is that? Well, based on our testing, we've come to find that attempting to do a Gray-Hat SEO approach with lower-quality links without first having some of the basic rules of trust in place with Google, will get a site Sandboxed, or at least heavily penalized. However, when basic level of trust exists, in age and content for example, a Gray-Hat SEO approach can quicken the ranking increase for a Webpage. Why is that? Well, when I talk about an organic-like approach, that's what I truly mean.

The approach will look like its somewhat organically generated in that you'll have a wide diversity of IP addresses, primary keywords, natural keywords, and generic linking terms. We'll discuss just how to do this in our strategies guide, but for the time being you should focus all of your energy on a fully organic approach. This is especially important if you have a brand-new domain name that you're trying to build rank for. Why is this important? Well, remember, Google doesn't want to see a domain name forcing its way up to the top of its SERPs. When it does see this, it will institute a penalty, and that listing will see its ranking drop down. At first, this won't be apparent however. Google creates a level of obscurity by first allowing a domain name to gain rank, but later chopping it down when it issues its algorithm updates to penalize the over-optimizers.

So, how do we get started? Well, this is going to be highly dependent upon your site's status with Google. If you have a domain name that's relatively aged and Google indexed it two or more years ago, and you've built up some authority over time, then you're going to approach things differently than you would a brand-new domain name. So, let's take the initial approach: a brand new domain name. Now, even if you've purchased an aged domain name, you're going to want to follow some of the initial steps to build authority. To do this, we're going to utilize authority Websites to build rank. Now, what's an authority Website? Well, if you think about building authority being the accumulation of rank for a site, an authority Website is a site that already has a high PageRank. What exactly is PageRank? An algorithm determines PageRank, which Google utilizes to attribute the importance of a Webpage to.

So what about PageRank? Why is it so important? Well, as you'll come to find in your SEO career, a high PageRank is one of the single and most solitary goals of any SEM. Since PageRank is so difficult to increase, and each notch up from 0 to 10 is exponential of the level below it, having a high PageRank takes significant effort. You'll notice in the proceeding image by Elliance, Inc., the following is attributable to the PageRank of Webpages:

- <u>0 – 2 PageRank</u> – These are considered below average PageRank Webpages. Having a 0 – 2 PageRank means that you're just starting out or have a very new Webpage with little trust in age, authority, and content. This is where the majority of PageRank lies for newer sites.

- <u>3 – 5 PageRank</u> – These are considered average PageRank Webpages. Having a PageRank of 3 – 5 is a good accomplishment. However, moving from 3 to 4 and from 4 to 5 becomes increasingly difficult. You have to ensure that you target the three spectrums of trust as best you can.

- <u>6 – 7 PageRank</u> – These are the above average Webpages on the Web. Achieving a 6 or 7 PageRank is incredibly difficult and it's attributed to some of the most popular Webpages on the Web. If you look at the proceeding image, you'll notice that 0 – 7 PageRank is at the very bottom of the mountain, where almost all the sites on the Web fall.

- <u>8 – 10 PageRank</u> – These are the elite sites on the Web. They're your Google.com, YouTube.com, Yahoo.com, and Facebook.com. So few Webpages fall into this category, and achieving this type of PageRank is incredibly difficult.

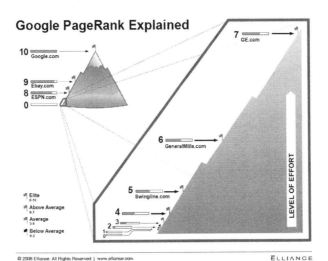

Google PageRank Explained

PINGING

Billions upon billions of Webpages exist out there. Google knows about most of them, but not all of them. And, in fact, it doesn't bother with crawling some of them, especially the ones with little to no PageRank. So, how do you go about getting Google's attention in the beginning? Every new site has an uphill battle to climb. You have to literally tell Google about links to your site and even your site itself. This is especially true when the links to your site are being created on sites that are not authority sites. When links are being created on authority sites, Google will quickly find those links because it crawls authority sites far more frequently the higher the PageRank of the site is. So, if you want to get Google's attention, you have to create links back to your site from sites that Google already trusts.

But, what about the times when you build links back to

your site from sites that Google might not find right away? Well, you need to ping those links to Google. By pinging links, you're letting Google know that they exist. And, even if it's an authority site, sometimes by pinging a link, you can be sure that it's crawled, expediently. If you don't ping the link, oftentimes you're unsure when the link will is crawled. And, it's not difficult to ping a link. As you'll come to find, the process is relatively simple and doesn't involve much effort. However, pinging is much more important when we're dealing with a large quantity of links. Now, as you're maybe aware of by now, Google banned engaging in link schemes. But, we'll look at just what a link scheme is as its defined by Google and what other options exist.

It's import to understand what a link scheme really is. Google goes into detail about what a link scheme is, but it remains a gray area. According to Google's Webmaster Guidelines, a link scheme is considered to be "Any links intended to manipulate PageRank or a site's ranking in Google search results may be considered part of a link scheme and a violation of Google's Webmaster Guidelines. This includes any behavior that manipulates links to your site or outgoing links from your site." Included in Google's definition of what a link scheme really is, contains the following bulleted items, which Google claims can "negatively impact a site's ranking in search results."

- Buying or selling links that pass along PageRank – Google claims that this definition would be for any link that's exchanged for money, goods or services, or links that are received in exchange of a "free" product. In essence, Google frowns upon any buying or selling of links because this is not a natural or organic approach. However, the gray area that would exist would be what specifically Google would consider as buying or selling links and just how it would determine this.

- Participating in excessive link exchanges – Again, a gray area here would be in the word "excessive" and just what Google considers being excessive. Of course, it can determine link exchanges by comparing and contrasting the outbound links and inbound links on any two Webpages that link to one another.

- Engaging in large-scale article marketing – This is an important one to keep in mind because Google doesn't like to see hundreds or thousands of links created every single day to an article that look unnatural and inorganic. It could help a Webpage or a domain get Sandboxed. So, you'll have to tread with care after creating your high-quality content not to fall into bad graces with Google.

- Using automated programs, services, or systems to create the links to your site – Now, this is an important point because Google is expressly forbidding any linking that is unnatural and inorganic. Plenty of systems on the Web exist to help you create unnatural links by the thousands, which is something that you need to be wary of. If you ever set about buying links or using software to create links in mass, you're going to run some high risks with Google.

- Non-editorial links – Google is essentially banning all links that are not the result of a natural and organic vouching. This applies to everything from paid advertorials with links from popular sites, to optimized links in press releases, and any other link that was generated unnaturally and inorganically.

It's important to keep these rules in mind any time you're not engaged in a fully organic approach. Google states that what the best way you're going to get "other sites to create high-quality, relevant links" to your own site is to "create unique, relevant content that can naturally gain popularity in the Internet community." And, if you recall my constant reference to high-quality content, you'll see why this is so important now. Not only is this important from a relevancy standpoint, but also from a linking one as well. Google knows that high-quality content is going to gain natural and organic links over time, so make sure that you create only good content.

So, where does pinging come into play with all of this? Well, anytime that you create links out there on the Web, you're going to want to tell Google about them. Google only crawls part of the Web every day, not all of it. Sites with low PageRank will not be crawled as often as sites with high PageRank, and that's where pinging comes into play. When you create links to your content, you're going to want to tell Google about them. We'll delve into a deeper discussion about pinging in the next course and just what strategies and tactics you can use to help foster the creation of relevant and high-quality links to your content on the Web, and inform Google of them in the process.

BUILDING AUTHORITY

Now that you know a little bit about how authority works, we can get started with building authority for your site. To build authority, as previously indicated, you have to work on creating as many high-quality links with high PageRanks as possible. Now, although thousands of authority sites exist out there on the Web, your job is going to be to build as wide and diverse a set of links as you possibly can. You don't want all of your links coming from the same few authority sites time after time. That's because Google likes IP diversification. It doesn't like to see all of the links coming from the same sites, but rather different ones, which indicates a much more organic linking pattern. It likes to see variety. And, the best way to build variety is to use as diverse a set of sites as you possibly can.

But, why do we use authority sites to help build PageRank for your own Website? Remember the discussion about trust and just how Google comes to determine trust? If you'll recall, I mentioned that you have to have a baseline level of trust already determined by the age of the domain name and the quality of the content. Once those two have been established, authority has to be built over time and using the help of other trusted sites out there on the Web. Remember, Google crawls and spiders the Web, linking from one site to the other. The way it finds other sites is by finding links on sites it already knows about. So, you have to do your best effort in order to get out there and create links to your site from sites that Google already trusts.

Now, for the most part, you're going to find this to be the most time-intensive part of your SEO work. Beyond just building the high-quality content that's required for a successful SEO campaign, you must also get people to link to that content as well. Because, when Google sees other trusted sites linking to your content, it draws the conclusion that the content is of some particular value. If it had no value, then no links would exist to that content. And, when Google sees links being created in an organic fashion from a very diverse set of sites, its algorithm increases the PageRank of that content over time. So, now that you know just how important it's going to be to begin with a successful link-building campaign, it's important to know where to start.

So, where do we begin? Well, below you'll find a list of authority sites that have high PageRanks with Google. These are sites that Google trusts and considers links from them to be important. If you'll recall the SEO Quake plugin that we used to determine how difficult it would be to rank for a given search term, you'll remember the sections that contained just how many Tweets, Likes, and Plus Ones a particular Webpage had. This is all part of the algorithm of trust through authority. When there are thousands of Tweets, Likes, or Google Plus Ones, Google's algorithm knows the importance of a piece of content. But, beyond those social cues that exist from social networking sites, other authority sites are important as well. Remember, Google is looking for diversity here.

So, in the list below, you'll notice not only the social networking sites that we've all come to know today, but also other authority sites that will allow you to build content and links. The list below contains the site names, their PageRanks, and a brief description of the type of content that can be created using them. It's important that you focus on these sites and creating trust through authority by building links and content. We'll get into some strategies in the next course, but for now, it's important that you take these sites and create a profile and account on each one in order to begin your trust through authority work.

1. Twitter.com (PageRank: 10) – Most people have a Twitter account. However, if you don't, ensure that you setup a public Twitter profile and you connect that to your public Facebook account so that updates on your public Facebook profile and Twitter account are tied together. When social media accounts are linked to one another, they become more powerful. That's because a link from a social media site itself is a very popular link since they have high PageRanks. When you link one social media site to another through their built-in profile settings, you're essentially creating a very powerful Link Wheel. A link wheel is a term used in SEO that essentially indicates Websites all linked to one another – Site A to Site B, Site B to Site C, Site C to Site D, Site D to Site E, then Site E to Site A – and in the middle is the site you're trying to promote. So, for example, if you want to move a Website to the top of

Google's SERPs for your keyword, link all the social media sites to one another, and on each of those sites ensure that you place a link to the homepage of your Website.

2. Facebook.com (PageRank: 9) – Facebook is the most important social media site you can setup a public profile on. Now, if you have an existing privacy-enabled profile on Facebook, then you should setup a public profile that won't be tied to your existing account. Even if you don't add any friends on this new public profile, it's going to be imperative to help clog up the first page of Google's search results for your name. And, if you're targeting your company's name, or your product's name, then you should setup a Facebook Business Page so that it will be indexed at the top of those search results.

3. Plus.Google.com (PageRank: 9) – Another very powerful social media tool for building, protecting, and repairing your reputation. Again, with Google Plus, it should be linked to your other social media profiles. And, the benefits of a Google Plus profile is that it allows you to create an unlimited amount of links with keywords to the sites of your choosing within your profile. To do this, simply click on the "Profile" tab in the top left of Google Plus, then click on the "About" link in the top-menu, and then scroll down to the links section. This is where you can add links to all of your other profiles and pages that you want to move up to your first page of Google search results.

4. Youtube.com (PageRank: 9) – Another one of the Web's incredibly high PageRanks, YouTube.com is another way to build authority for any Webpage or domain. Links that you create on YouTube will rank very high, and will aid you in moving other Webpages up in the search ranking. To post links, just create a "Channel," go to "My Channel," and start posting the links. Google will find these incredibly quickly, and the link will move up the search engine rankings quickly. However, aside from the boost you can give other links by linking to them from your YouTube channel, the YouTube profile itself is a very powerful one to have. Again, this will serve to help build authority over time. No matter what domain you're trying to promote, create a YouTube profile for it. If you're doing it for your company, your product, or anything else, create a YouTube Channel within your YouTube account and name it to whatever keyword you're targeting.

5. LinkedIn.com (PageRank: 9) – Most people know about LinkedIn and have a LinkedIn profile. But, if you don't have one, it's important to set one up. With a PageRank of 9, this is an incredibly popular domain to utilize when building rank for anything on the Web. Once you're all setup, you can also share posts and links, allowing you to further build up the SEO value, and subsequent PageRank, for any Webpages or pieces of content that you may have on the Web.

6. Xing.com (PageRank: 9) – This is a social network similar to LinkedIn. It has 13 million business professionals worldwide and growing. Since this has such a high PageRank, you should make creating a profile on Xing.com a priority. Then, link to it from your other social networks. Use Google Plus to create an unlimited amount of links with any keyword to all of your other social media profiles.

7. Vimeo.com (PageRank: 9) – Vimeo is a video sharing site. You should create a profile on Vimeo. You can also connect Vimeo with your Facebook account, Twitter account, Tumblr account, LinkedIn account, and Google Plus account. Again, this will only further enhance that link-wheel effect of having all of your social media profiles tied to one another. Furthermore, if you're inclined to upload videos, Vimeo is a great way to socially share them and create high SEO value. When your profile has many very popular videos in it, its PageRank increases more. Keep in mind, just because the homepage of Vimeo.com has a PageRank of 9, it doesn't mean that your profile on there will. PageRank changes for each page, even on a domain. However, on a domain that's extremely popular PageRank will start relatively high. This is an important concept to keep in mind.

8. Wordpress.com (PageRank: 9) – The most popular blogging platform on the planet, a profile, and blog that's setup on the Wordpress.com domain, will allow you to create high-quality links

to any Webpage. Make sure that you name your blog with the company or keyword you're trying to promote. So, if you name your blog "iPhone 7 Rumors," then your blog would be located at iphone7rumors.wordpress.com. Of course, you should also change the title of the blog to your primary keyword as well. This way, not only is the keyword in the URL, which is very important, but also on every page of the blog no matter what you post.

9. Pinterest.com (PageRank: 8) – This is an extremely popular photo-sharing Website with a high PageRank. Create a profile page on this Website and link your Facebook, Twitter, and Google Plus profiles to create a link wheel effect. You can do this by going into the Account Settings section and scrolling down to the "Social Networks" part. Again, doing this creates a solid link wheel. A link wheel created from profiles of social media sites is incredibly powerful. When one links to the other, and to the next one, and so on, the SEO structure is virtually impenetrable. But, don't expect these to move up in ranking overnight. It will still take weeks until Google does a deep re-indexing of its databases for the biggest improvements to be realized. Sometimes this can still take up to 90 days.

10. Tumblr.com (PageRank: 8) – Tumblr is an incredibly popular blogging platform, which was recently purchased by Yahoo for $1.1 billion

dollars. The platform allows you to post updates that include links, photos, quotes, chats, videos, and audios. More importantly, it has a very high PageRank. Also, links posted onto your Tumblr account will help to considerably push up other content that you're trying to rank on Google's SERPs.

11. Slideshare.com (PageRank: 8) – Slideshare is an incredibly popular site where individuals can post Word documents or PowerPoint Presentations that are highly visible for SEO purposes. Your Slideshare profile is also a high PageRank piece of the Web that will allow you to move it up the ranks to the top of your keyword search, quickly and effectively. However, Slideshare can also help you to rank Word documents that you may want to release into the world in an effort to build more high-quality content. Those Word documents must not be spammy or be advertisements, but rather, something that provides value to people. You should always provide value when releasing content on the Web so that your efforts don't look to forced or insincere.

12. Plurk.com (PageRank: 8)

13. Reddit.com (PageRank: 8)

14. Scribd.com (PageRank: 8)

15. LiveJournal.com (PageRank: 8)

16. Myspace.com (PageRank: 8)

17. Lifestream.AOL.com (PageRank: 8)

18. Blogger.com (PageRank: 8)

19. Typepad.com (PageRank: 8)

20. Delicious.com (PageRank: 8)

21. Slashdot.com (PageRank: 8)

22. StumbleUpon.com (PageRank: 8)

23. About.me (PageRank: 7)

24. Bibsonomy.org (PageRank: 7)

25. Deviantart.com (PageRank: 7)

26. Diigo.com (PageRank: 7)

27. Instapaper.com (PageRank: 7)

28. Newsvine.com (PageRank: 7)

29. Storify.com (PageRank: 7)

30. Scoop.it (PageRank: 7)

31. Bitly.com (PageRank: 7)

32. Tagged.com (PageRank: 6)

33. Skyrock.com (PageRank: 6)

34. Hi5.com (PageRank: 6)

35. Kaboodle.com (PageRank: 6)

36. App.net (PageRank: 6)

37. Kippt.com (PageRank: 6)

38. Jumptags.com (PageRank: 6)

39. HubPages.com (PageRank: 6)

40. GetPocket.com (PageRank: 6)

41. Folkd.com (PageRank: 6)

42. Webshare.co (PageRank: 5)

43. LinkaGoGo.com (PageRank: 5)

44. ZooTool.com (PageRank: 5)

45. Sonico.com (PageRank: 5)

CREATING AUTHORITY CONTENT

One of the most important parts of the process to building authority is also building authority content. What do I mean by this? Well, if you'll recall our conversation about trust you'll remember just how skeptical Google is about increasing the SEO presence for Webpages on domains that it doesn't already trust. However, if that same content were created on a domain that Google already trusts, it's an entirely different ball of wax. Why is that? Well, when content comes from authority sites such as YouTube.com, Wordpress.com, Tumblr.com, or any of the other authority sites out there on the Web, Google will automatically trust that content more because those sites have built a track record of trust over time. So, one of the important parts of your work here is going to be to leverage authority sites by creating content that links back to existing content that you have.

What do I mean by all of this? Well, by creating unique, engaging, content that provides tremendous value on authority sites that already have trust with Google, and linking that content with your primary keyword to a similar piece of content that's also unique, engaging, and provides tremendous value, you'll solidify an important relationship of trust. When Google sees this happening, your Webpage will immediately increase in PageRank. But this isn't easy to do. It takes a considerable amount of time to build this type of content on both an authority site and your own site, link them together, and do this consistently over time. But, when you do this, the bond of trust grows stronger and stronger. This is one of the best organic strategies to building trust through authority with Google. Now, this won't satisfy the trust through age component. If you don't have an aged domain name, there's not much around that unless you purchase an aged domain name. However, even without an aged domain name, this technique, when conducted consistently over time, will considerably increase the PageRank for any domain and Webpage.

In the proceeding image, you'll see a graphical representation of just what this type of technique would look like. As you'll notice in the image, you'll see that the unique authority content is linking to unique content on your own site that share a similar primary keyword. Now, this can also be an LSI keyword as well, which would make it look more organic to Google. But, either way, it's important that the content is on the same topic and the primary keywords are similar. And, the link must be coming from the authority site to your own Webpage, and not the other way around. Especially when that authority content becomes shared and linked to by lots of other Webpages, and that same authority content is linking to your own Webpage, the prominence and PageRank of your domain name increases dramatically.

Content Marketing

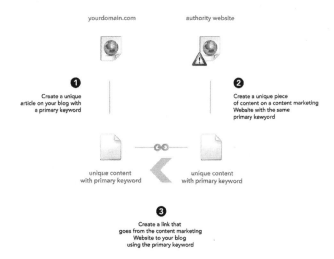

This particular technique is also known as content marketing, and it's one of the best-kept SEO techniques in the book. In today's competitive SEO environment, especially with all the recent algorithm adjustments that have taken place with Google, content marketing is going to be one of the optimal methods to propelling your site forward on Google's SERPs. It allows you to quickly build up PageRank by leveraging the sites that Google already trusts. And, as long as you create incredibly unique content that provides tremendous value and is engaging, this technique is going to propel you to the top of SERPs. We'll go more into this strategy in the next course, but for the time being, it's something that you should begin implementing and practicing as soon as possible.

OTHER COURSES

I hope that you enjoyed reading the material covered in this course. Hopefully, you've come to understand the fundamentals of the SEO industry, and you now have a solid foundation for continuing your SEO career. Remember, that your SEO work doesn't end here. This should have provided you with a general direction and understanding for SEO, but the subsequent courses are going to help really propel your career forward.

Be sure to continue your SEO education and look at some of the other courses that are available in this series. From building niche Websites, to content marketing, video marketing, and everything in between, we'll cover some of the advanced strategies for propelling you forward in the SEO world. Remember, there's nothing better than free organic traffic, and there's no other better way to develop that free traffic than truly understanding the world of SEO.

APPENDIX
SEO TERMINOLOGY

Aged Domains – An aged domain is a domain that has been indexed by Google at least two or more years ago and it's a critical component of any successful SEO campaign. Google penalizes new domain names, making it very difficult to rank any keywords at the #1 position, or even on the first page of search results for that matter, in the beginning. Purchasing or having an aged domain will be one of the critical factors in your success for ranking a site high for any given keyword.

ALT tags – Also known as alternative tags, these tags appear within the HTML <img> tags that present the alternate data to the search engines to provide a description of what the image is. For optimal search engine rankings, you should have at least one image ALT tag that correlates with your site or page's primary keyword.

Backlinking – Likely to be your biggest undertaking when it comes to SEO, backlinking is the effort involved with creating hyperlinks that link back to your Website.

Black-Hat SEO – Black-Hat SEO is a term used to describe SEO tactics that are not compliant with Google's Webmaster Guidelines. Black-Hat SEO techniques are frowned upon by the search engine industry. Examples of Black-Hat SEO techniques are things like trying to hide keywords within HTML comment tags, or trying to cloak pages.

Breadcrumb – A navigational aid used on Websites, breadcrumbs not only allow users to quickly jump through informational sections on the site, they also provide high SEO value by allowing the search engine spiders access to quickly navigate and spider through a site, indexing data faster and more efficiently.

Cloaking – This is a technique that delivers different content to the search engine spiders than it does to real human visitors. The cloaking technique is oftentimes used to mask the real content, or change the real content of a page, and make it appear differently to a search engine spider. This is considered a Black-Hat SEO technique, and while it is sometimes used for legitimate purposes, it is oftentimes used to display pornographic material to real human visitors, while only displaying non-pornographic material to a search engine spider.

CPC – Cost-per-click, or CPC, is a term used in online paid advertising to indicate click-through percentages. The cost per click is calculated by diving the number of clicks with the total amount spent on the advertisement. For example, if you spent $100 on an ad, and 200-clicks were received, the CPC would be $0.50 cents.

CSS – Cascading Style Sheets, also known as CSS, is a Style Sheet Presentation Markup Language that is used to position elements, layouts, colors, fonts, images, and essentially construct a Webpage. While CSS is used primarily in styling HTML Web pages, it is also used to style XML and other documents.

Dofollow Links – Dofollow links are an attribute associated with an HTML hyperlink that tell a search engine to continue to link through to the site, disseminating some of the site's important link juice. Dofollow links are very powerful types of links that work well when pointed to your site. When a search engine sees a Dofollow link it continues linking through to the site, passing part of the SEO link juice that would have been offered to that page had the link been a Nofollow link.

Duplicate Content – In the search engine world, content is king, but duplicate content is the court jester. Copying large chunks of content to your site is one of the biggest no-nos in the industry. The search engines will figure it out eventually and you will be demoted in the rankings. If you're going to do SEO right, make sure all the content is high-quality and unique content that's well researched.

Headings – HTML headings are blocks of code that are placed around certain words, styling and providing a certain level of prominence in the overall page structure. Heading tags range from <h1> through <h6>. However, in the modern SEO world, the first three hold the most importance. Tags <h1> through <h3> should all contain the primary keyword spaced throughout the page with the <h1> and <h2> tags being above the Website fold.

Internal Link – Internal links are links from your page's content to another page or section on the same domain.

Keyword – A keyword is a word or phrase that is used to optimize a Website or Webpage. Selecting keywords is one of the most important tasks in SEO work, and selecting the right keywords in the outset can either make or break you. It's important to note that the keyword "Miami vacation" and "Vacation Miami" will produce different search results, so the order and positioning of the words within the phrase is just as important.

Keyword Density – The keyword density is the number of times a keyword appears on a page in relation to the total number of words. Optimal keyword density ranges from 2% to 5% with anything considerably over 5% being construed as SPAM, and anything considerably lower than 2% being construed as not keyword rich enough, and thus less relevant. It's important when writing your content that your primary keyword is evenly distributed throughout the page, making sure that it appears in the first and last paragraph of the content, as well as evenly spaced throughout the balance of the words.

Keyword Stuffing – Keyword stuffing is the over-usage of a keyword in content or meta keyword tags, something that used to be popular many years ago but is now frowned upon as a Black-Hat SEO technique. Keyword stuffing is achieved in various different ways which include: placing the phrase multiple times within the meta tags while combined with other words in different combinations, applying the same color to the keywords as the background making them invisible, using the <noscript> tag, and using CSS z-positioning. All of these practices will get you demoted and sometimes de-indexed by search engines like Google.

Long-Tail Keyword – A long-tail keyword is a keyword that has a minimum of at least 5 words and any maximum number of words. Long-tail keywords are used by marketers trying to target a specific niche, question, or topic, which produce near similar results to a broader search term of lessor keywords but may have higher competition. Long-tail keywords are a great way to rank at the top of search engine results for terms that may otherwise be more difficult to rank for.

Link Bait – Link Bait refers to content that is created in order to garner as many links to it as possible. Since backlinks are one of the primary drivers of SERP positioning, many SEO efforts include the creation of content with the primary goal to get as many links back to that content as possible.

Link Farm – A link farm is a group of sites that all hyperlink to one another, back and forth, in an oscillating fashion. While link farms used to be advantageous, they don't have large relevancy today since the two-way links make it confusing for search engines to determine which site is the vendor, and which is the promoting site.

Link Juice – This is the SEO linking power of a page, and usually refers to the combined sum of the link power of all the pages linking into it. You'll hear the term link juice referenced when quantifying the power of a certain link or a page that those links lead to.

Link Pyramid – A Link Pyramid used to be a very powerful form of Off-Site SEO backlinking that involved the creation of a linking structure that is extremely powerful. These are no longer popular today since Google now primarily qualifies these as link schemes. Link Pyramids generally have three tiers: a bottom tier with low-level links, a middle with medium-level links, and a top level with high-level EDU, GOV or other authority links. The bottom links link to the middle, the middle links link to the top, and the top links link to your site.

Link Sculpting – When you implement attributes to links to affect their behavior in how search engines interpret them, you're engaging in link sculpting. The most common form of link sculpting is using the Nofollow or Dofollow link sculpting forms. The Nofollow links tell a search engine not to follow a link, thus leaving the link juice on the page, while a Dofollow link tells a search engine to continue on to follow that link, thus disseminating the link juice to the next page.

Link Wheel – A Link Wheel is a form of linking that links one site to another while also linking back to your site as well. The links flow in a sort of wheel format with the spokes being links back to your site in the center. When done correctly, and not forced, a link wheel can be a powerful form of SEO boost for your Website. And, the most effective forms of link wheels are organically fashioned ones that utilize social media platforms as their linking mediums.

LSI – Latent Semantic Indexing is a semantic technology for grouping together similar words or phrases that closely resemble others through the usage of mathematical computations. LSI is a way that Google and other search engines help to determine what Web listings should appear at the top of SERPs when keywords don't exactly match one another. Understanding LSI and its implications when creating high-quality content is going to be critical to your success in SEO.

Meta Keywords – Meta keywords are part of a set of meta tags that appear in the header of Websites. Meta keywords used to be prominently used in search engine rankings, but have no interpreted value of importance today. Instead of using meta keywords, search algorithms now use other tags such as heading tags, site content, keyword density, and backlinking keywords to determine search engine rankings.

Meta Description – The meta description tag is one of the meta tags that are still used by search engines to display search results. This along with the title tag is used to display the name and description of the link on SERPs to the user searching for information.

Nofollow Links – Search engines spider the Web looking for information, and in turn ranking the relevance of sites in its indexes. Nofollow links are an HTML attribute associated with hyperlinks that tell a search engine to not follow the link, stopping the search engine's traffic at that page, almost like a dead end. Nofollow links are paramount to ensuring that your own Webpage is optimized to the highest level possible by not allowing the link juice to pass through it.

Off-Site SEO – Off-Site SEO are the methods and practices of performing SEO work that happen away from the site itself. Off-Site SEO mainly involves the use of heavy backlinking, social media shares, authority site content creation (i.e. squidoo.com, youtube.com, etc.), article spinning, and so on. Off-Site SEO is a very labor-intensive part of the SEO trade, and.

On-site SEO – Any work that is done on the Website to increase the effectiveness of its SEO is considered On-Site SEO. This includes any HTML work, content creation, internal linking, setup, keyword distribution, and other related efforts.

Page Title – The HTML page title is the descriptive site title detail that resides within the page's <title> tags. This information is displayed by the search engines and is used in ranking the site on the SERPs. A good page title tag should be descriptive but not superfluous, and should accomplish its goal in around 70 characters (the cut off point for most SERPs), with the use of the primary keyword.

Pinging – Pinging is a technique that notifies the search engines to go out and seek data from a URL. This is required because a lot of the link building that is done happens on low, or no PageRank sites that are not visited often, or at all by the search engines. When a search engine is pinged to go out and index a URL you can be certain that the hyperlink to your site or to a link that's pointing to your site, will be found and indexed.

Panda – The Google Panda is a change in the algorithm for Google's search results that was released in February of 2011. The effects of Panda were to demote low-quality sites and promote sites with high-quality well-researched information. The effects of this release were widespread, making huge shifts in positioning on SERPs forcing some businesses to lose large volumes of search traffic, while others were able to gain it.

PageRank – One of the most important descriptors of a Webpage, the PageRank is a Webpage's rank in relevancy on the Internet, ranging from 0 to 10. Sites like Facebook, Twitter, and Google's home page achieve PageRanks of 9 and 10, while lower trafficked sites have lesser PageRanks.

Penguin – The Google Penguin was a major update released to Google's algorithm on April 24th, 2012, which began to demote visibility of listings on SERPs that violated Google's Webmaster guidelines and employed Black-Hat SEO tactics such as cloaking, keyword stuffing, and the creation of duplicate content.

PPC - Pay-per-click advertising, or PPC, is a form of paid search engine advertising that marketers use to get their message out to the masses on a large scale very quickly. PPC ads show up on the right side of SERPs and are now being implemented on Facebook, YouTube videos, and more recently on sites like Twitter.

PPV – Pay-per-view ads, or PPV, is a type of advertising that is utilized by marketers to distribute ads to a user base that has expressly agreed to receive those ads. An example of this is free software downloads, or online services such as Pandora that use PPV ads to display advertisements on a periodic basis while providing a free service.

Referrer String – Referrer strings are used in affiliate and Web marketing to pinpoint campaigns and where a lead or referral came from. This is important to some marketers running paid advertisements to be able to gauge the successes of their various efforts throughout the Web. Web programming dictates that after the Web page name, a question mark can indicate the start of any variables that may be appended to a URL, thus resulting in a Referrer String.

Robots.txt – This is a file that resides in the root directory of your Website, that provides instructions to search engines on any folders, or files that it shouldn't index. Most people don't want search engines seeing all files on their sites such as administration files, or other files that contain sensitive information.

RSS Feed – A Rich Site Summary (RSS) feed, is a standardized format that allows for the automatic update and syndication of content on sites that have frequent changes, and entries such as blogs and other news sites. The RSS feed format provides a standard in formatting that allows ease of redistribution of either full or summarized data, metadata, and publishing information.

Sandbox – Google Sandbox Effect is an effect that happens when a newly formed domain name's link juice is not fully weighted due to filtering from Google in order to prevent spammers from reaching the first page in SERPs by registering multiple domain names quickly and actively promoting them.

Search Algorithm – A formula devised by brilliant minds that weighs and considers multiple factors when reaching a determination for search result PageRanking. The Google search algorithm combines many factors including the aged domain factor, Website link popularity, On-Site SEO elements, and Off-Site SEO elements. No one outside of Google knows the exact current algorithm and the total weight of each of the factors that are taken into account or precisely how they impact search results, but there are very good guidelines available.

SEM – SEM is the business of search engine marketing, the industry that search engine optimization specialists fall under. SEM is used to refer to not only SEO efforts, but also paid search engine marketing efforts as well.

SERP – Search Engine Ranking Pages, also known as SERPs, are the end listing results pages of queries to search engines. SERPs will generally include a title and brief description of each listing related to the keywords searched, along with a link to that content. In SEO, the goal is to dominate the first page of SERPs.

Sitemap – A sitemap is a page that's created to aid browsers in crawling a site. A sitemap provides a hierarchical link structure of pages on a Website that are accessible and permissible to be crawled.

Social Media – Social media is a term that refers to the types of sites that have increased in popularity in the past several years that base themselves on end user interactions in a social and collaborative format. Examples of such popular sites are Facebook, Google Plus, and Twitter.

Spider – A Spider is a Web-robot that's instructed to go out and crawl the Internet for data used for the purposes of Website indexing and rankings. Google has multiple spiders that it sends out, some that are dedicated to deep-indexing the Web, others for more periodic updates to Web content. And, even others for algorithm adjustments such as the Google Panda and Google Penguin.

Website Fold – The Website fold is the section of the Website that is viewable to the natural eye before getting cut off by the browser and forcing a user to scroll. The Website fold will vary from screen resolution to screen resolution. However, it's typically 600 to 850 pixels down from the top of the browser.

White-Hat SEO – White-Hat SEO techniques are those that follow the rules and standards of the SEO world and adhere to Google's Webmaster Guidelines. White-Hat SEO techniques, while more time-intensive, offer the largest long-term gains for your Website's ranking on SERPs. These techniques include quality-content creation, proper On-Site SEO configuration, and organically looking Off-Site SEO linking.

Made in the USA
Middletown, DE
25 March 2015